ORNAMENTAL WATERFOWL

The Authors

Lt.-Col. A. A. Johnson, M.C.
Formerly
Proprietor of The Priory Waterfowl Farm, Ixworth, Suffolk

W. H. Payn, M.B.E., F.L.S., M.B.O.U.
Author of *The Birds of Suffolk*

PLATE 1 *Frontispiece*

Painted by Roland Green

A GROUP OF ORNAMENTAL DUCKS

IN FOREGROUND ARE DEPICTED A PAIR OF MANDARINS, WITH BAHAMA PINTAILS
ON THE RIGHT AND ON THE LEFT A DRAKE TEAL; A PAIR OF CHILOE WIGEON ARE
SEEN SWIMMING BEHIND THEM WITH COMMON PINTAIL DRAKE IN BACKGROUND

ORNAMENTAL WATERFOWL

A Guide to their Care and Breeding

BY

LT.-COL. A. A. JOHNSON. M.C.

AND

W. H. PAYN, M.B.E., F.L.S., M.B.O.U.

TEXT DRAWINGS BY ROBERT GILLMOR

THIRD EDITION

PUBLISHED BY THE SPUR PUBLICATIONS COMPANY
Hill Brow, LISS, Hampshire

THIRD EDITION 1974

© A. A. JOHNSON and W. H. PAYN 1974

ISBN 0 904558 02 9

Previously published by H F. & G. Witherby Ltd.

Set in 10 point Times and printed in Great Britain by
Calabre Printing Limited, Liss, Hampshire

CONTENTS

ILLUSTRATIONS

INTRODUCTION

Many people have the idea that in order to keep ornamental ducks, geese and swans successfully, it is necessary to provide them with a large sheet of water upon which to swim, or an extensive park or pasture in which to roam.

This is far from being the case, and in the following pages we hope to show, not only that wild ducks and geese at any rate, can be kept in perfect health on quite small ponds, in gardens of modest size, or in paddocks or orchards, but also that to keep a pair or two, only the smallest amount of water is required, no more, in fact, than would provide a home for a few goldfish.

Since the appearance of the first two editions of this book, there have been very considerable improvements in the methods of feeding and propagating waterfowl. There has also been a great increase in the numbers and variety of species available. We have endeavoured to bring all information in the book on these and other points up to date.

ACKNOWLEDGEMENTS

A number of friends who are also waterfowl enthusiasts, have helped us with suggestions and information for this book; others have kindly provided photographs for use in it. We are particularly indebted to :

Messrs R. Burn, S. H. Charrington, Derrick Lord, Frank Mosford, R. E. M. Pilcher, G. R. Roper-Caldbeck, B. Turner, and J. W. Williams; to Major H. M. Peacock, Captains Hamilton Scott and C. R. Peacock, Christina Sanday, the Hon. Peter Strutt and Pamela Harrison.

Our grateful thanks are also due to Messrs M. O. J. McCarthy, M.R.C.V.S., and J. A. Dall, B.Sc., M.R.C.V.S., of the Animal Health Trust, who have given us invaluable help with Chapter 7.

We must also acknowledge our indebtedness to Jean Delacour's *The Waterfowl of the World,* for information on the incubation periods of some of the rarer geese and swans, and to Robert Gillmor for the attractive new drawings in the text.

CHAPTER 1

STARTING A COLLECTION

WATERFOWL AS A HOBBY

It is probably true to say that waterfowl—by which we usually mean wild ducks, geese and swans—are among the most popular of all birds not only with naturalists and sportsmen but also with the general public. Indeed this is hardly surprising, for few birds display at once such diversity of shape and brilliance of plumage, such lively and engaging habits or such perfect trustfulness once their confidence has been gained.

In comparison, too, with most other kinds of birds which are kept in captivity, waterfowl have the great merit that under suitable conditions they can be given almost complete liberty in garden, paddock or orchard, where their charming ways and decorative plumage add greatly to the beauty and interest of their surroundings.

Among the thousands of people who every year visit one or other of our Wildfowl Trusts or who can be seen any fine day in summer or winter feeding and admiring the ducks, geese and swans in the public parks in London and other large cities, there must be many who feel that they would like to keep a few ducks or geese themselves but who are perhaps deterred by the idea that the difficulties would be too great.

There is, in fact, no reason at all why anyone who is interested in waterfowl should not keep at least a pair or two, even if they have only the smallest of gardens or nothing more than a back yard. We know a wildfowler who keeps quite a large collection of geese and ducks in the garden of his council house.

DEVELOPING A WATER GARDEN

Naturally, anyone who already has an orchard, meadow or garden containing a natural pond, starts off with a great advantage, but those who have neither garden nor pond to start with need not despair; almost any piece of ground can, with a little trouble and skill, be fenced in, suitably planted with shrubs, and provided with an artificial pool which will prove quite adequate for the needs of a few ducks or geese. And what immense pleasure the cheerful bustling presence and bright plumage of these birds will give throughout the year to old and young alike !

A pair or two of ornamental ducks cannot fail to add charm and interest to any garden or pool, no matter how beautiful it may be already and this is particularly the case in winter or spring when the colourings of the drakes stand out at their brightest against the still water or the green of a lawn. Nor need anyone be afraid that a few ornamental ducks will do damage in a flower garden; one of the authors of this book keeps some fifteen pairs of ducks and a pair of Barnacle Geese loose in a garden of about an acre and a half, and they do little or no damage.

Only when too many birds are kept in too small a space do lawns or plants suffer from their attentions. In later chapters will be found a description of some of the more easily-acquired ducks together with hints on their good and bad points if kept at liberty in a flower garden.

We are often asked whether ornamental ducks are likely to kill or injure goldfish. The answer is definitely "no". Except for the "saw-billed" ducks, the Merganser, Goosander and Smew, which live very largely on fish and are seldom kept in captivity, none of the ducks or geese take the slightest interest in live fish of any kind, though they might eat the corpses of dead ones. However, it would not be advisable to try and keep ducks and goldfish together in a very small pool, owing to fouling of the water.

The first and most essential requirement for anyone who proposes keeping waterfowl in his garden or orchard must be to provide adequate fencing to prevent his birds from straying and to protect them from the attention of foxes, dogs, and vermin in general. If ducks are to be kept, their enclosure must contain at least a small stretch of permanent water—even though this be no more than a concrete pool which, with a little skill, can be made to look quite ornamental. Most of the wild geese will live in health and happiness with no more water than is provided by an old tin bath sunk in the ground, though they will probably not breed under such conditions unless the water is changed very often.

Beside permanent water, the enclosure must also contain some trees or shrubs to provide shelter and shade, as well as nesting cover, also a certain amount of short grass. The latter is essential if geese are to be kept, though ducks can do without it. Advice on fencing and planting a waterfowl enclosure and the construction of artificial pools will be found in the next chapter.

Once the garden or enclosure has been adequately fenced against intruders and provided with water and shrubs for shelter, there comes the question of stocking it—in fact the would-be waterfowl-keeper should begin to make plans for this purpose well in advance. For the complete beginner the only really satisfactory method is to buy one or more pairs of hand-reared and pinioned birds from a reputable breeder, of whom there are a number in this country. A pinioned bird is one which has been rendered permanently flightless.

SOURCES OF BIRDS

Some wildfowlers like to keep alive any wing-tipped ducks and geese which they may bring down while shooting and these birds will usually settle down in captivity and become fairly tame, but they will generally not breed and are never as satisfactory as hand-reared birds.

It is also possible to start a collection by hatching and rearing ducks from eggs which have been purchased or picked up in the wild.

AVOID OVERCROWDING

As we have said, the number of waterfowl that can be kept in health depends on the amount of space that can be provided for them. Generally speaking, a small pool of about six to eight square yards is ample for one or two pairs of the smaller ducks, provided they also have a fair amount of space in which to roam.

It is a great mistake to over-crowd waterfowl, for if this is done the grass is soon eaten off, and the ground and water become foul. Under such conditions the birds will never look their best. It is also useless to expect ducks and geese to breed if too many are crowded into a small enclosure. So do not be too ambitious at first, start with a few pairs and add to them gradually as space allows.

Most of us would prefer to see our birds full-winged and able to fly about, but this is a most risky proceeding with rare and valuable birds which may stray away and get lost or shot.

It is sometimes possible to keep some of the less valuable species full-winged by pinioning only the females. The drakes will then usually return to their mates after their morning and evening flights.

The smaller ducks, that is to say the several species of Teal and perhaps the Carolinas and Mandarins, can be kept free-winged in a completely enclosed aviary and this is a most excellent way of showing off these graceful and swift-winged little birds. They soon become adept at flying round inside their aviary with no risk to themselves. Quite a small pen would be sufficient for a pair of Teal or Garganey, though the handsome Mandarins or Carolinas would require more space. If branches are provided the Carolinas and Mandarins will perch freely on them and ornamental pheasants can also be kept with the ducks to give added colour and interest.

Although we have stressed the importance of providing some form of enclosure in which to keep pinioned ducks and geese, we must say that we know of a few people—large landowners and farmers—who have found that under particularly favourable conditions, they are able to give their birds complete liberty to wander where they will—on foot, but there must always be a risk, under such conditions, of losses from the stray dog, fox or otter or even from a human predator.

SPECIES AVAILABLE

The complete beginner to waterfowl-keeping may wonder what species to start with, and he cannot do better than to go and see a fellow enthusiast's collection or to pay a visit to the Zoo and look at the waterfowl on view. He will soon decide which species most appeal to him and having ascertained their names he can then make arrangements to purchase a pair or two from some breeder.

Meantime we give below a list of some of the more attractive and less expensive ducks which in our view are particularly suitable for beginners.

Carolina	**Red-crested Pochard**
Mandarin	**Pochard**
Pintail	**Tufted Duck**
Garganey	**Wigeon**
Bahama Pintail	**Chiloë Wigeon**
Cape Teal	**Cinnamon Teal**

(By including the Chiloë Wigeon, Bahama Pintail and Cape Teal, which have no eclipse dress, some birds in the collection would always be in colour.)

4

PLATE 2

Photo : *Richard Burn*

A SMALL GARDEN POOL AND ENCLOSURE 5 YARDS BY 10 YARDS PROVIDES AMPLE LIVING
SPACE FOR TWO PAIRS OF SMALL DUCKS

PLATE 3

Photo : S. H. Charrington

Photo : C. R. Peacock

TWO EXAMPLES OF WATERFOWL ON LARGE NATURAL PONDS

CHAPTER 2

FENCING, PLANTING AND POND CONSTRUCTION

ENCLOSURE ESSENTIAL

When valuable pinioned waterfowl are to be kept at semi-liberty in garden or orchard, a fence of some description becomes an absolute necessity, both to prevent the birds from straying and to protect them from intruders.

Anyone living in a fox-free neighbourhood, who is satisfied that dogs are unlikely to be a menace to his ducks and geese, need only erect a low fence, some three to four feet high, of light wire-netting, sufficient to keep his birds from straying.

This fence need not be unsightly. It can usually be planned, with a little skill, to run behind a hedge or group of shrubs in such a way as to be almost invisible and when it is in view it can be disguised quite effectively by the application of a little dark green paint.

However, if foxes or dogs are likely to be troublesome, it is absolutely essential to erect a more substantial fence round the garden or paddock where it is planned to keep ducks and geese.

This need not be a difficult or expensive undertaking. A satisfactory and inexpensive fence can be made of one-inch "chain-link" fencing three or four feet high, with a second tier of four-feet three-inch mesh galvanized wire-netting joined to it on top, to make a total height of about seven feet, of which the top is bent outwards.

7

The fence must be about seven feet in height to prevent foxes or dogs from jumping over, and the overhang at the top will also make it impossible for them to climb over the wire.

The fence will, of course, have to be supported by wooden or metal uprights, and metal angle-iron stakes will be found particularly suitable for this purpose as they can so easily be driven into the ground to the required depth and once in place will virtually last for ever.

Another form of dog and fox-proof fencing, which waterfowl-keepers have employed with success, consists of cleft-chestnut fencing about five feet high with a backing of light wire-netting to prevent anything pushing through between the uprights and more netting along the top. Some form of electrified wire along the top will also help to discourage the most determined raiders, but if the fence is well constructed to start with, such extra precautions should not be necessary.

It is important to remember that both foxes and dogs may try to burrow under the wire, which must therefore be buried at least a foot below ground and be very firmly pegged down.

If the fence should run alongside or through a pond, it is important to make sure that the netting rests on the bottom of the pond, as otherwise some of the ducks when diving may find their way under the wire and escape.

Whatever materials are used, the fence must be made sufficiently strong to prevent a determined dog from forcing its way through and sufficiently high to prevent it climbing or jumping over.

A fence that meets these requirements will generally keep out cats as well.

CONSTRUCTING A POND

Once the fencing of the waterfowl enclosure has been completed the next operation is the construction of a suitable pond or pool. If the enclosure has been designed to include a piece of natural water, such as a pond or stream, it will only be necessary to make such alterations to the banks as will enable the future inmates to walk in and out with ease.

On the other hand, ducks and geese love sunning themselves on a sloping bank, particularly in winter-time when the sun's rays are weak, and the north bank of any natural pond should therefore be altered where possible to provide an easy slope free of undergrowth where the birds can congregate in comfort.

Steep banks to a pond or stream are not ideal for waterfowl but they do provide shelter in rough weather.

Too much shrubbery or undergrowth along the banks should be discouraged as it provides harbour for vermin such as rats, but a few evergreen shrubs can be left overhanging the water to provide useful shelter and wind-breaks in times of frost and snow.

If a stream or brook flows through the enclosure, it can easily be dammed-up or diverted to form one or more small ponds or pools which can be made to look even more attractive than natural ponds, as it is easier to maintain a constant water-level in them.

When no natural water is available within the enclosure, one or more artificial pools will have to be made, of any desired shape or form. They can be of a formal rectangular or circular shape of any required dimensions or they can be given an informal, irregular outline which, with skilful planting, can be made to look most natural.

The construction of an artificial pool presents no great difficulties. A site must be chosen if possible on ground which allows a slight fall into a natural ditch or else to an artificial soak-away into which a drain can be constructed from the bottom of the pool. This will make draining the pool for the purpose of cleaning and refilling an easy matter. If a drain from the bottom of the pool cannot be made for any reason it will be necessary, when changing the water, to fall back on the old and well-tried method of using a piece of rubber hose to syphon it out.

If it is found possible to incorporate in the design of the pool an outlet drain to facilitate emptying, this outlet pipe should be cemented into position low down on one side of the pool when it is being constructed and a water-tight plug of some kind inserted in the pipe on the inside.

We have seen a large screw-top bottle, such as a beer or cider bottle, used for this purpose with great success. The bottom of the bottle is first sawn off with a hack-saw and the open end thus made is fitted into the end of the piece of piping which is to carry the water away from the pool, while the neck is left to project slightly inwards and almost flush with the bottom of the pool. The bottle itself must be firmly cemented into place. All that is then required is to screw the stopper home before the pool is filled and to unscrew it when for any reason it has to be emptied. Fibre-glass pools of various shapes and sizes are now on the market and these have been found quite satisfactory for ducks and geese. They can be sunk into the ground quite easily and require no maintenance.

9

Having decided on the site, the proposed outline of the pool, whether formal or irregular, should be marked out on the ground by means of pegs and string, before digging begins.

Remember that a pool which is partly raised above ground-level will, obviously, require less digging, but it will also need to have thicker concrete walls and can seldom be made to look as attractive to the eye as one constructed at ground-level.

Whatever shape the pool may be, it is quite unnecessary to make it too deep. A depth of not more than three feet at the centre will be found ample for the requirements of all diving-ducks, while surface-feeders will be satisfied with a depth of eighteen inches to two feet.

If the finished pool is to be raised, say, six to nine inches above ground-level, the soil which is taken out of the hole can be retained and used later on to provide a neat slope up to the concrete edge.

A CONCRETE POND

One of the most important points to be remembered when a concrete pool is under construction is that the bottom and sides of the hole must be made very firm indeed before concreting begins. They must also be as level as possible to avoid stresses and strains on the concrete when the pool is finished and filled with water.

If the bottom and sides of the excavation are of gravel or chalk they should be rammed very firm before the concrete is applied, but in the case of a clay soil which is likely to shrink or crack in dry weather, it is most advisable to put on top of the clay a layer of dry ashes about four inches thick and well rammed down before concreting begins. On a sandy sub-soil a base of well-rammed brick, stone or clinker should be constructed. It will of course be necessary to provide some form of rough wooden "shuttering" to support the sides until the concrete is dry.

As so much will depend on the completed pool being permanently watertight and strong, only the best materials should be used. The concrete should be made of cement, sand and shingle in the proportion of one part cement to two parts sand and two parts shingle by volume—very well-mixed and applied rather moist. Mix sufficient concrete to cover the bottom in one operation and wait till the bottom is dry before starting on the sides. Concrete sets hardest when it has dried slowly, so in hot weather freshly laid concrete should be covered with wet sacking.

The thickness of the concrete on the sides and bottom of the finished pool should not be less than six inches and it is always advisable before filling the pool to give the inside surface a final "priming" of liquid cement applied with a brush.

The sides of the finished pool should not be vertical but should be sloped off gradually towards the centre, or they can be made slightly concave, which makes it easier for the birds to climb ashore.

Remember that the ducks will be going in and out of the water all day long and will be liable to make the soil at the edge of the pool muddy and unpleasant. This can be avoided by making a neat edging about a foot wide all round the pool of either paving-stones or bricks or coarse shingle about three or four inches deep.

MAKESHIFT POND

When only a few ducks are to be kept in an aviary or small enclosure, one or more old stone sinks buried up to the rim and filled with water will prove quite sufficient for the needs of the inmates. Such a sink will also be found quite adequate for a pair or two of small geese which do not require much water for bathing. However, a small fibre-glass pond is likely to lend itself to more attractive landscaping.

To supply these artificial pools and sinks with water, it will be found much more convenient to provide a piped supply from the mains rather than to have to fill them by hand.

PROVIDE NATURAL COVER

Once the enclosure has been adequately fenced and provided with a natural or artificial water supply, it will probably be found necessary to do a certain amount of planting of shrubs and plants, not only to make the enclosure more attractive to the eye but also to provide shelter and nesting places for the inmates.

Trees and shrubs should be planted in groups, leaving plenty of space between so that the ducks can be seen to the best advantage. Most coniferous trees are ornamental and at the same time provide shelter in bad weather. If they grow too big they can always be uprooted and smaller specimens planted to take their place. Norway Spruce and Larch are particularly suitable, as well of course as such select trees as *Cedrus atlantica glauca* and *Cedrus deodora*.

Of the shrubs, lauristinus, box and Portugal laurel, and the various species of juniper and bamboo are not only wind-resistant but also look tidy and ornamental at all times of the year. Among plants, clumps of "Pampas-grass" and periwinkle provide particularly good nesting cover. Most of the taller irises as well as several of the larger senecios—notably *S. wilsoniana* and *S. pulcher*—look tidy when not in flower and are not eaten by ducks and geese. Clumps of iris, astilbes, etc., can be planted right at the edge of an informal pool to break the outline— in fact the possibilities are endless.

A few flowering shrubs and trees such as members of the berberis family, buddleias, flowering crabs and thorns as well as weeping willows and red-twigged osiers will all help to add colour and interest to the enclosure throughout the year.

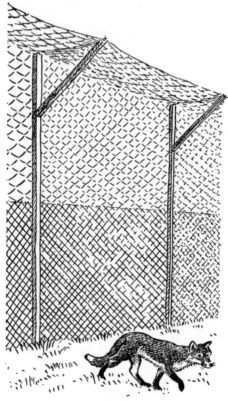

"Foxed"!

The grass should be kept short as it looks so much better than when it is allowed to grow long and tangled, and if geese or a few of the grazing-ducks such as the Common, American or Chiloë Wigeon, are included in the collection they will usually do all that is necessary to keep the herbage short.

ISOLATION PENS

When the waterfowl enclosure is being designed and built, the opportunity should be taken, at the same time, of constructing one or more quite small pens nearby which can be used for rearing young stock, for invalids, and for newcomers. The latter sometimes take a few days to settle down and get used to fresh surroundings and new food, while newly-caught wild birds can easily die of starvation if turned straight out into a large enclosure where they can creep away and hide. A small pen only a few square yards in area will prevent this.

The foregoing recommendations for the design of pools and the planting of enclosures apply equally well—though of course on a reduced scale—to covered aviaries in which it is planned to keep full-winged Teal or other small ducks.

For keeping down grass and weeds in large paddocks and enclosures sheep such as Soay or Jacob's four-horned sheep are recommended. They are hardy, tame easily and require very little extra feeding. Rabbits and guinea pigs are also useful as grass mowers for small pens and enclosures.

CHAPTER 3

GENERAL MANAGEMENT OF THE COLLECTION

GETTING THEM TAME

The principal aim of anyone who keeps ornamental waterfowl should always be to win their complete confidence and trust from the start. Ducks and geese which take food fearlessly from the hand, or which tug trustingly at their owner's legs when they consider they are getting too little attention, cannot fail to give more pleasure and enjoyment to their owners or to strangers who come to see them, than birds which flutter and flap away in all directions as soon as anyone approaches.

And it is usually so easy to win a bird's confidence. Hand-reared waterfowl are naturally trustful of those they know—embarrassingly so at times—and even wild-caught birds often prove surprisingly easy to tame. One of us possesses a wild White-fronted Goose which ate bread from the hand within six weeks of being captured and which now likes to travel about sitting on the front seat of a motor-car.

The surest way to any bird's heart is through its stomach and the person who normally feeds them will soon become so familiar to the waterfowl that they will crowd round his or her feet with complete fearlessness to await their meal. Soon the bolder ones will begin to snatch food from the hand and then it is only a step or two until they will allow themselves to be stroked and even lifted up by hand as they gobble their bread and corn.

While some species of ducks and geese are naturally more confiding than others, like human beings they vary individually, some are naturally bold, others unalterably shy and wary.

14

PLATE 4

Photo : Brian C. Turner
THIS ARTIFICIAL POOL OF VERY PLEASING DESIGN IS IN A TOWN GARDEN

PLATE 5

Photo : R. E. M. Pilcher
THIS ARTIFICIAL POND IN ITS ATTRACTIVE SETTING SHOWS WHAT
CAN BE DONE WITH SKILL AND IMAGINATION, AS POND AND ENCLOSURE
WERE MADE FROM A PLOUGHED FIELD

Photo : F. Mosford
YOUNG BAHAMA PINTAILS ON A SIMPLE ARTIFICIAL POOL

PLATE 6

Photos : Christina Sanday

TWO TYPES OF FENCING, SHOWING WIDE TURN-OVER AT TOP

17

PLATE 7

Photo : Lt. Col. A. A. Johnson

A GARDEN POOL IS MADE STILL MORE ATTRACTIVE BY THE PRESENCE OF ORNAMENTAL DUCKS

Every waterfowl-keeper should bear in mind at all times the two golden rules:

1. Always talk to your birds, using the same call or tone of voice, whether you are feeding them or merely walking among them. They will soon come to associate your voice with good things.

2. Never hurry or flurry: always move quietly and deliberately when approaching or walking among your waterfowl and if possible never appear among them in some striking new garment. They are conservative creatures, deeply suspicious of the unfamiliar.

KEEP FEEDING SIMPLE

Generally speaking, wild ducks and geese are hardy and long-lived and are easily kept in good health with only the smallest amount of attention. In fact they can be treated much like domestic poultry. They should be given two feeds a day, one consisting of "free-range" poultry pellets and one of wheat or mixed corn, on which simple diet they should remain in good health throughout the year.

Modern chick, pheasant or turkey "crumbs" for young birds, and pellets for growers and adults have been so much improved in recent years that they now provide a balanced diet perfectly suited to almost all waterfowl.

If preferred, ducks and geese can be fed, in place of pellets, on a mash consisting of cooked potatoes and household scraps, dried off with meal but the best egg-laying and fertility results are probably achieved by using high-grade poultry or turkey pellets.

In severe weather a little cod-liver oil can be given and some crushed maize added to the corn, and when green food is scarce a handful or two of alfalfa (lucerne) meal should be mixed with the mash.

Windfall apples, pears and plums, as well as chopped sugar-beet and acorns are enjoyed by all geese and most species of ducks which also like lettuces, dandelions, sow-thistles, lawn mowings and, of course, water-weed of all kinds.

Remember too that ducks, geese and swans require a regular supply of limestone, oyster-shell grit or sand; this can be put down in a trough or in a heap on the ground. An occasional poultry tonic can be added to the food; it all helps to keep the birds in good health and therefore in good plumage.

PROVIDE WEATHER PROTECTION

Waterfowl, like most birds, hate wind and draughts and must be given protection against them at all times. If the shrubs and trees already growing in the enclosure are insufficient, a screen of osier or wattle hurdles, about three feet high, should be erected either round the sides of the enclosure or on the banks of the pool.

In very severe weather it is a good plan to put some straw on the ground for the ducks and particularly the geese whose feet may become frostbitten if they have to sit out all night on ice or snow.

Unless the enclosure is very sheltered, straw bales should also be provided as wind-breaks in severe weather.

GUARD AGAINST PREDATORS

The waterfowl-keeper must be constantly on guard against the depradations of vermin which can cause losses not only to young birds but also to adult stock. If suitable fencing has been provided the birds should be safe from dogs and foxes, but unless they are kept in a completely enclosed aviary, the smaller ground vermin such as stoats, weasels and rats may cause trouble at times.

Weasels are probably only a danger to very young ducklings and goslings, but stoats will kill adult ducks if they can catch them away from the water, while rats are insatiable hunters of young ducklings and we have known them to kill adult birds as large as Gadwall.

Rats can, of course, be gassed in their burrows or poisoned, but one of the best ways of dealing with them, as well as with stoats and weasels, is to keep a number of tunnel-traps set continuously throughout the year at strategic points round the outside of the waterfowl enclosure, as well as in any drain-pipes through which a rat or stoat might pass. These traps will catch the majority of stoats, weasels and rats before they have had time to do any damage.

Though daytime attacks by stoats and weasels can be troublesome they are usually spasmodic, for these ferocious little animals are wanderers and are unlikely to take up residence in the vicinity of a garden, but rats will, if allowed, establish themselves in buildings and banks near the waterfowl. One rat will attract others and soon there will be a colony. This must never be allowed. As soon as the presence of rats is noticed, a vigorous campaign with poison, traps and gas should be launched against them and not given up until the last rat has been accounted for.

In some parts of the country otters can be a serious menace to pinioned waterfowl which are quite defenceless against their under-water attacks, and there have been cases of otters attacking birds as large as geese and even swans.

Fortunately otters are seldom plentiful and the trouble is usually caused by a stray otter which has come upon the waterfowl during one of its cross-country journeys.

A fox-proof fence will generally prove too much for an otter also, though the latter is a good climber and where its attacks are feared it will be found advisable to reinforce the sides of the enclosure with sheets of tin on which an otter's claws cannot obtain a grip.

Apart from hedgehogs which will readily make a meal of a nestful of eggs, the only other animal likely to cause losses among the waterfowl is the domestic cat, which is one of the worst enemies of the bird-keeper. The night-prowling puss is quite capable of getting into a pen or coop and killing not only young ducklings but adult birds as well. We have had a valuable Falcated Teal drake killed and eaten by a cat and have also lost Gadwall, Bahama Pintail and Common Teal in the same way.

The best way to protect ducklings and goslings is to make sure that cats cannot get into the enclosure. Cats cannot climb up wire-netting itself but they will climb up the posts which support it, particularly if the posts are of wood, and we have found it an effective deterrent to tie a large bunch of gorse, holly or butcher's broom to all posts up which a cat might try to climb, or to fix a semi-circular fan of tin or wire-netting at right-angles to the post and about three-quarters of the way up it.

Winged-vermin such as owls, crows and magpies can be troublesome at times. The Tawny or Brown Owl is a powerful bird which will sometimes hunt by day and is strong enough to carry off a half-grown duck, while all the crow tribe are great egg-stealers. The latter can be trapped or shot without great difficulty, but it is well to remember that most of their raids take place very early in the morning when most of us are usually still in bed.

Last, but by no means least, on the waterfowl-keeper's list of foes is the Moorhen. This spiteful and quarrelsome bird can be a great nuisance if only because it eats the food put down for the ducks. But it will also bully and sometimes injure adult ducks, and if a pair of Moorhens are allowed to breed on the same pond or stream as waterfowl they are liable to kill every duckling which comes near their nest. We have seen a pair of Moorhens kill off a whole brood of young Carolinas in a few hours without the mother duck being able to protect them in any way.

When dealing with attacks by vermin, prevention is always better than cure, and for some years we have made use of a preparation called "Renardine". This is a strong-smelling liquid which can be applied to posts and pieces of sacking hung on the outside of the waterfowl enclosure and is said to keep foxes away. It can also be sprinkled on the grass and bushes surrounding ducks' nests when the smell will definitely help to conceal the presence of eggs or sitting bird from prowling rats or stoats.

It may appear from the foregoing that the life of pinioned ducks and geese is one continuous hazard. This is not really the case: with ordinary care and luck casualties should be few —certainly among adult stock. Once a suitable enclosure has been provided, they really require little more protection than is normally given to a flock of domestic poultry or ducks.

CHAPTER 4

NESTS AND EGGS

ENCOURAGE BREEDING

The nesting season is the busiest as well as the most interesting time of the year for the waterfowl-keeper who should always try to encourage his birds to breed, whether it be to increase his own stock, to replace losses or to produce a surplus for exchange with other breeders.

Unfortunately some wild geese do not breed freely in captivity. Even hand-reared geese are not likely to lay fertile eggs until they are three years old and most wild-caught geese will generally not lay at all, or not until they have been in captivity for many years. Conditions must be exactly to their taste before geese will think of nesting. All that can be done to encourage them, is to provide them with plenty of space, good grazing and freedom from disturbance.

Wild duck generally pair in the autumn and on fine sunny days during the winter we shall frequently have had the pleasure of watching the drakes indulging in their elaborate and charming courtship display, but as the days lengthen we shall see the first real signs of breeding activity when the paired birds start to wander off together in search of nesting sites.

At first it is all rather casual and spasmodic, but by early April many of the ducks will have made up their minds where they are going to nest and soon, if all goes well, we shall find ourselves with the fascinating, if sometimes rather exasperating task of searching the long grass and undergrowth for the first eggs.

Not all ducks in the collection are likely to breed, however. Unless conditions exactly suit them, many wild ducks are shy breeders in captivity, though some of the more robust species will try to nest under the most adverse conditions.

NESTING FACILITIES

Their main requirements are plenty of cover and peace and quiet. A duck hates being bothered and interfered with by a strange bird of its own or another species. In fact, unless they have plenty of space, it is better to keep pairs of the same species separate during the breeding season. Overcrowding is to be avoided at all costs.

Nevertheless, given plenty of concealment such as rough grass and shrubs, ducks will nest quite happily in close proximity to each other—sometimes within a few feet—without interfering with each other in any way. If undergrowth in the enclosure is sparse, added shelter can be provided by clumps of broom or evergreens stuck in the ground to form a canopy or by loose piles of bracken or hedge-trimmings.

For ducks such as Shelducks, Carolinas and Mandarins, which normally nest in burrows or holes in trees, artificial nesting sites must be provided. Shelducks will readily use an artificial burrow constructed from a length or two of six-inch drain-pipe sunk below the surface of the ground and with a small nesting chamber at one end. This should have a close-fitting lid of wood or slate which will allow easy access to the nest if it is proposed to remove the eggs or to watch the progress of incubation.

Carolinas and Mandarins will also use such nesting sites, though they prefer a small box or barrel with a hole in the end, fixed a few feet high in a tree and provided with a small ladder for getting up and down.

There is no need to make very elaborate or expensive nesting boxes. Hollow logs or old metal drums or chimney pots can easily be adapted to serve the purpose. One of our Shelducks nested year after year in an old oven turned on its side with a piece of drainpipe as an entrance tunnel.

Excellent nesting sites for Shelducks can also be constructed from bales of straw. Ducks are very adaptable if they want to breed and sometimes choose surprising places for their nests.

The important thing is to bring them into breeding condition by a varied diet containing plenty of protein. A diet which consists wholly of, say, potatoes and grain is not conducive to good breeding results.

Once they come into breeding condition the waterfowl will start looking round for nesting sites that take their fancy. With Mandarins and Carolinas it is the drakes which seem to do the prospecting, leading their mates about and calling attention to suitable places by running in and out of the entrance and twittering in a high state of excitement.

The ducks sometimes take several weeks to make up their minds, running about in the meantime in great agitation, but once they have decided which nest-box they are going to use, they settle down quite contentedly, merely visiting the box once or twice a day until they are ready to start laying.

Because of their habits there is seldom much difficulty in deciding beforehand where Carolinas and Mandarins are going to nest, but it is a very different thing where ducks such as Teal, Pintail, Gadwall and Shoveler are concerned. Like most ground-nesting ducks, they conceal their eggs most skilfully in long grass or piles of dead leaves and, in a large enclosure or garden, it is quite a business to find them before incubation begins. However, with practice and observation, there are plenty of clues to be followed.

Firstly, the paired ducks will have started looking about for a nesting site some time before they are actually ready to lay and if we see the pair—for the drake always accompanies his mate—regularly frequenting some particular part of the garden or enclosure, this will give us some idea as to the probable nesting area.

WATCH FOR NESTING SIGNS

A few days before she actually lays, the duck will make one or two "scrapes", that is to say, she hollows-out with beak and feet a small depression under a tuft of grass or in a heap of leaves and this is quite noticeable if we know what to look for. She may make several of these "scrapes" within a few yards of each other and in a day or two one of them will contain the first egg. The duck does not cover her eggs until she has laid three or four, when she usually starts to conceal them beneath a layer of grass, leaves and twigs and later on, just before she begins to incubate, with down which she plucks from her own body.

It is far easier to find the nest during the first few days when the eggs are exposed and catch the eye, rather than later on when they are covered over, for then it takes a very sharp and experienced eye to detect the nest.

Ducks usually lay between daybreak and ten o'clock in the morning. When they are missing during these hours it is sometimes possible to follow their tracks to the nest in the dew. Their mates, too, give the show away by hanging about in the vicinity of the nest while the duck is laying.

Under the most favourable conditions it is often difficult to find every nest and some individual ducks are very clever at misleading possible watchers. They start off purposefully in one direction, but no sooner are they out of sight in tall grass or behind a shrub, than they double back on their tracks and find their way to the nest by a most roundabout route.

The waterfowl-breeder should always try to locate all the nests he can. If he plans to leave the ducks to incubate their own eggs, he can protect them a little against ground-vermin by sprinkling "Renardine" round the nest or against crows and other winged-vermin by carefully adding a little to the overhead cover if necessary.

DAILY COLLECTION OF EGGS

If the eggs are to be incubated artificially they should be picked up daily and kept in a cool place until the clutch has been completed. At least three or four eggs—dummies for preference—should be left in the nest till the duck has finished laying.

If it is in a safe place, all the eggs can be left until the clutch is complete and some breeders also recommend allowing the duck to incubate the eggs for a few days before lifting them.

This brings us to the all-important question of how the ducklings are to be hatched and reared. In our opinion there is no doubt whatever that the best way is to hatch the eggs under bantams or in incubators.

In captivity most species of duck prove themselves extremely incompetent mothers, probably because they do not get enough privacy. They will usually sit well and hatch their clutch successfully, but as soon as the young are strong enough to travel, they start to drag them aimlessly about all over the place, through the long grass and up and down the banks of the pond and seldom allow them long enough to rest or feed. The mother ducks are probably made over-anxious by the presence of other adult waterfowl: and not without reason, for many ducks and drakes which have no young of their own seem to go out of their way to chase and molest any ducklings which come near them.

PLATE 8

Photo : Richard Burn
NEST-BOX FOR CAROLINAS AND MANDARINS

Photo : Richard Burn
THIS NEST-BOX MADE FROM AN OLD OVEN AND A PIECE
OF PIPING, HAS BEEN USED FOR MANY YEARS BY SHELDUCKS
AND CAROLINAS

PLATE 9

Photo : Pamela Harrison

A MAJESTIC PAIR OF RED CRESTED POCHARD

28

The result in any case is that within a very short time the majority of the brood have generally been lost, tired out from continually trailing about after their mother, with insufficient time to feed and rest.

It is exceptional for any pinioned duck, if left to her own devices, to rear more than one or two of her brood and generally she loses them all within a few days. If she can be kept by herself with her brood in a small pen, she may succeed in rearing them, but in the long run it is far better to take her eggs and give them to a hen or bantam to hatch. In this way she may be persuaded to lay a second clutch.

Some people consider that if a duck is never allowed to hatch and try to rear her ducklings she is liable to lose interest in the whole thing and may not nest at all. Although we do not consider this likely to happen, the instinct to breed being renewed year by year, we have found it a good practice to give ducks which have perhaps laid a second clutch after the first has been taken, one or two common eggs such as those of Mallard or Call Duck, and allow them to hatch these as a reward for their labours. We consider this particularly important in the case of wild geese, which can be given the eggs of a domestic goose to keep them happy.

CHAPTER 5

HATCHING AND REARING

INCUBATOR OR BROODY?

Until quite recent years breeders of ornamental waterfowl used broody hens or bantams almost entirely for hatching and rearing their young ducks and geese, though the latter were often left to the care of the parent birds.

Sometimes this method proved very satisfactory but on the other hand results were often so disappointing, owing to the vagaries of hen or parent goose, that breeders began to experiment with the use of incubators. After a period of trial and error it has been found that, provided one or two simple rules are followed, incubator hatching has many advantages, particularly where ducks' eggs are concerned.

When many eggs have to be incubated, much time and labour is saved, while there is no danger of eggs being broken or ducklings crushed at hatching time by a restless or clumsy broody.

The one vital thing to remember is that the eggs of waterfowl always require a very much higher level of HUMIDITY during incubation than do the eggs of domestic poultry and this applies particularly when incubators are in use.

The ideal method, however, is probably a combination of the artificial and the natural and all those who aspire to breed waterfowl should keep a flock of hens and bantams which can be used as broodies or foster-mothers at need.

Those who only expect to hatch a clutch or two of eggs will in any case be well advised to stick to the old and proved method with broody bantams which can generally be relied upon. The eggs of swans and geese are probably best left to the care of the parent birds, though the eggs of the latter can also be hatched under hens.

For all kinds of duck smaller than the Shelduck a bantam foster-mother is ideal, and the best bantam is one which has "silkie" blood in it. Pure "silkies" are very good indeed, but we have found that their plumage is less resistant to wet than a first or second-cross which retains all the "silkie's" broodiness and can cover the young ducklings more efficiently. It is easy to tell if a bantam contains "silkie" blood by looking at its feet: "silkies" and first-cross "silkies" have an extra toe on each foot and the feet themselves are usually lead-coloured. Do not use a broody with feathered legs, or else clip the feathers before putting her down.

We have also found that the Sumatra Game or Sumatra cross makes a very satisfactory sitter but it is essential to make sure they are really sitting closely before being put down on live eggs.

The waterfowl-keeper who has a flock of hens or bantams upon which to draw for foster-mothers will almost certainly find that some of them have gone broody before any ducks' eggs are available for setting. These birds should be cooped in the normal way so that they can be used again later on, but by the end of March one or two should be in the nesting boxes ready for the first clutches of ducks' eggs which will probably be Carolinas', followed in early April by those of Shoveler, Pintail, Gadwall, Red-crested Pochard and so on.

PROVIDING NEST BOXES

Each broody hen must be provided with her own nesting box, large enough to enable her to turn round comfortably but not too large or she will not cover the eggs properly. A small, cramped nest will result in broken eggs.

The bottom of the box should contain a sod of turf with a slight hollow scooped out of the centre and large enough to hold the clutch of eggs, and this hollow should be filled with a mixture of soft straw and hay and the whole nest then covered with a layer of oat straw. The turf will help to conserve moisture and must be thoroughly damped before incubation begins.

The broody hen or bantam should be put down on dummy or hard-boiled eggs several days before her proper clutch is given her. This will ensure that she is quite at home and sitting "tight": if she is a restless or nervous bird, as some are, she can be rejected altogether or kept in reserve for less valuable eggs.

Before being put down on eggs the broody should be thoroughly dusted with insect powder.

Each nest-box should be provided with a hinged front which, when closed, will ensure that the sitting bird is in darkness or semi-darkness and she should be left absolutely quiet. Some people believe in placing the nest-boxes outdoors directly on the ground, but we prefer to have them all under cover in an airy shed or barn where the birds can be let off to feed whatever the weather may be.

Once a day each broody must be carefully lifted off her eggs by hand or allowed to walk off by herself. She must be given a handful of good, sound wheat—not soft food—and as much water to drink and grit to eat as she requires. There should also be readily available a pile of bonfire ash or leaf-mould in which the bird can take a dust-bath if she feels inclined. This is where having the nest-boxes under cover proves such an advantage, since the broodies can be taken off their eggs in any weather, and several can be allowed off at once instead of having to be tethered individually as is the case when birds are sitting in the open.

During the first week of incubation, the broody should not be allowed off the eggs for more than five or ten minutes at a stretch, but the period can be extended as incubation proceeds and during the last week no harm will come to the eggs if the hen is off for half an hour.

Actually most broodies know quite well how long they should be off their nest and they will go back unaided once they have fed and stretched their legs.

We have already mentioned the great importance of correct humidity for the eggs during incubation. In a natural state wild ducks' eggs are usually laid on the damp ground, in addition to which the sitting duck's plumage is always wet when she returns to the nest from feeding and bathing and some of this moisture is naturally transferred to the eggs and keeps the shells and the membrane within the shells soft.

But the broody hen's plumage is not wet when she returns to her eggs and if we do not provide the necessary moisture the shells will become very hard and the membrane within "leathery".

When ducklings die in the shell, or only manage to get half out, the trouble is almost always due to insufficient moisture during incubation, with consequent tough shells out of which the ducklings cannot break their way.

After the first week of incubation, whenever the broody is taken off to feed, her eggs should be liberally sprinkled with water and during the last few days before hatching they can even be dipped completely for a few minutes in a bowl of tepid water. The turf in the nest-box should be well damped once or twice a week and the eggs should also be turned by hand frequently.

If all goes well and the eggs are fertile the first faint stirrings of life should be audible within the eggs some twenty-four to forty-eight hours before they are due to hatch. These will be followed by the first chipping of the shells.

A period of about twenty-four hours generally elapses between the first chipping and the final hatching of the egg, though this period varies with individual clutches and to a certain extent with the different species of duck or goose. If the broody has sat closely and the eggs have not been allowed to chill they should hatch uniformly and on the correct day according to the incubation period of that particular bird. These incubation periods are given on page 99.

However, individual clutches do vary considerably in their hatching periods, some hatching twelve hours before they are due, while others go a day or two over their time. On no account should unhatched eggs be discarded until they are at least three or four days overdue and show no signs of life. In any case the precaution should have been taken of testing all eggs with a strong light at about the tenth day of incubation to ascertain whether or not they are fertile. An infertile egg will appear perfectly clear when a strong light is held behind it while a fertile incubated egg will be more or less solid and impervious to light.

Until the eggs are well chipped it is safe to allow the foster-mother off to feed in the usual way, but she should never be allowed off once the eggs are actually hatching, or the half-hatched eggs and newly-hatched ducklings may be crushed when she returns to the nest. She will take no harm if left undisturbed for twenty-four hours. The less she is interfered with the better; some people cannot resist constantly lifting up the broody to see how things are proceeding underneath. This will only worry and distract the bird who generally knows her job better than her owner.

Unless the broody is very quiet and reliable and in any case when small and valuable eggs are being incubated, it is a wise policy to complete the hatching of chipped eggs in a small incubator, after which the ducklings can be transferred to a moster-mother or back to the bantam mother.

EARLY DAYS

When the ducklings are all hatched and dry, the broody can be taken off to feed and stretch her legs, but she should then be allowed to return and brood them for some hours. At this early stage they are still very weak and will be warmer and safer in the nest-box than in a coop. But care must be taken to see that any strong and precocious duckings cannot get out of the box and become chilled. This is one of the reasons why the broody should be put down in a nest-box only just large enough for her requirements.

While the bantam is still brooding her young in the nest a coop and small wooden-sided run with a wire-netting top should have been got ready to receive her. The coop should rest on a board covered with dry sand or leaf-mould or chaff, but not on the bare ground, and should be placed on a sheltered lawn or even in a light and airy building. On no account should the run be placed on long, rank grass.

If the ducklings are to be started indoors we have found it an excellent plan to suspend an infra-red lamp over the pen in which they are confined. In this way a dozen or more ducklings can be given to one bantam and though she may not be able to brood them all, the lamp will help to keep them warm, while she will teach them to feed and look after themselves generally.

When the ducklings are dry and strong, they should be moved with their foster-mother into a coop.

Now comes the testing time, for the first week or so of a duckling's life are the most difficult. Two things are absolutely essential to success: to keep the ducklings warm and dry and to persuade them to eat readily. One would think that the latter, at any rate, should be easy, but this is certainly not always the case. It sometimes proves extremely difficult to persuade such ducklings as Teal, Shoveler, and Carolina to start feeding freely.

ENCOURAGE BIRDS TO FEED

It is no use just putting the food down in front of them and hoping for the best. We must make sure by actual observation that the ducklings are eating, otherwise in two or three days we shall find them beginning to die one after the other until the whole brood will have been lost—a most distressing event which has happened at one time or another to most waterfowl-breeders.

Ducklings can often be persuaded to feed by sprinkling a little food on their backs which the others will try and pick off. They can also be given live food such as meal-worms or gentles which will attract them by wriggling.

34

Sometimes young ducklings are restless and given to jumping up the side of the coop or run. This is a bad sign as they frequently refuse all food when in this frame of mind. There is little to be done, except to confine them for a time in a very small space.

Young ducklings do best on a varied diet consisting of chopped hard-boiled egg, dry "quaker-oats", brown bread-and-milk, varied with maggots, small chopped worms and water-weed. The more insect food that can be provided the better, at any rate during the first week or two, though unless conditions are particularly favourable for obtaining this kind of food, the sooner the ducklings can be got onto a standard mash the better. It is staggering what a lot of worms a brood of, shall we say Pintails or Shelduck, can put away at a sitting and still ask for more!

From the start, a small quantity of high-grade game "crumbs" should be put down for the birds in shallow dishes. They will soon take to them, after which most other foods can be reduced gradually and finally stopped altogether. We now rear most of our broods of ducklings quite successfully on turkey crumbs alone.

All food should be put down in small, shallow pans just out of reach of the foster-mother, except during the first day or two when she should be allowed access to the food so that she can encourage the ducklings to eat it.

Water should be provided sparingly at first, with a stone or two in the container to prevent the young ducks getting in to swim, but as they get stronger they can be given more water to paddle and bathe in. They like their food rather moist. The more sunshine the ducklings can get the stronger they will grow, though plenty of shade must also be provided to prevent any risk of sunstroke.

While she is in the coop the foster-mother should be given a good feed of wheat and maize once a day and should be allowed out frequently to stretch her legs. She will also need drinking water.

WATCH FOR PROGRESS

It will soon be obvious whether or not the ducklings are thriving. If, at four or five days old, they look sleek and plump and are to be seen constantly round the food-tins, they are doing well and barring accidents most of them should be reared successfully, but if they look thin, hump-backed and draggled, with overgrown beaks and messy tails the chances are that they will die.

There should be no check to their growth during the first fortnight, for it is during this period that they build up their reserves of strength preparatory to growing their feathers. It is a bad sign if the ducklings spend a lot of time under the hen and worse if they are constantly squeaking, for a squeaking duckling means a hungry, dissatisfied duckling.

If all goes well, it is remarkable how fast the ducklings will grow. At three weeks of age the first feathers appear and at six weeks they should be completely fledged except for the wings. Long before this, if the weather is mild, they will have become independent of their foster-mother, preferring to sleep outside the coop on warm nights, but it is a good plan to leave the bantam with the brood until they are fledged. In a wild state some ducks—notably Tufted Duck—are said to become independent of their mother at a much earlier age.

CHAPTER 6

PLUMAGE AND MOULT

RATE OF PROGRESS

Under favourable conditions the growth of a young duckling is very rapid indeed. Three weeks from the day of hatching the first feather-quills should begin to appear on crown, shoulders, breast and tail and at six weeks of age the bird should be fully-fledged except for the wing-feathers which require a few weeks longer to grow and harden sufficiently to enable the duck to fly.

Goslings and cygnets also grow very fast—and on little more than a grass diet at that—but being larger birds they take longer to come to maturity and some species retain their juvenile plumage until they are nearly a year old though most young geese are fully-fledged at 9–10 weeks of age.

Most ducks acquire their adult plumage during their first autumn, after a complete body-moult of the juvenile feathers, the original wing-feathers alone being retained until the late summer of the following year.

However, a few species, notably Shoveler, Teal and Gadwall among British ducks make the moult from juvenile to adult dress a more leisurely process, spread over most of the autumn and winter. The young drake Shoveler is seldom in complete adult plumage until it is nearly a year old, while on the other hand Mandarins, Carolinas, Pintails and most of the diving-ducks should be in almost full colour by their first Christmas.

SEXING THE BIRDS

Until the males begin to assume their conspicuous adult dress the members of a brood of young ducks all look very much alike and the beginner to waterfowl-keeping may well wonder how he is to tell the drakes and the ducks apart.

Admittedly this is not always easy and requires a certain amount of practice, but anyone with an observant eye should soon learn to distinguish between the sexes with reasonable certainty even when they are no more than seven or eight weeks old.

To start with there is the difference in size; most young drakes being slightly larger and more stocky in appearance than their sisters. Then, in the case of such ducks as Mallard, Teal, Pintail, Shoveler and Gadwall, where the juvenile plumage is a mottled brown rather similar to that of the adult female, a careful examination will show that the young drake's head is darker and less striped on top, that the feathers between its shoulders are more heavily pencilled and that most of the feathers on the back and rump have *narrower* buff fringes than in the case of the young duck.

The colouring of the beak of the two sexes will also be found to differ if only slightly and in the five species already mentioned practically all the females develop at an early age a number of small, dark spots near the nostrils. A difference in size between the sexes is usually noticeable among young Shelducks, the females also showing more white at the base of the bill. This holds good with practically all the Shelduck species.

In the case of the diving-ducks, where the sexes have different coloured eyes, the colouring of the iris of the young drake will begin to show at an early age, long before any difference in plumage can be detected. Careful inspection will also show quite early in life that the colouring of the beak of the young drake Rosybill and Red-crested Pochard is brighter than that of the young duck.

Finally there is the difference in voice. Until they are approaching maturity, the young males of practically all species of ducks are almost completely voiceless, while on the contrary the young females soon develop a rather feeble quack. This is a most useful guide when trying to sex a brood of ducks.

Young geese and swans are a very much more difficult proposition and it usually takes an expert to distinguish the sex of young stock, basing his opinion probably on differences in size and voice. All waterfowl can of course be "sexed" at an early age by physical examination of the vent.

Most adult waterfowl—be they swans, geese or ducks—have only one moult a year, but in the case of the males of many species of duck from the Northern Hemisphere, there is a second moult into what is known as the "eclipse plumage". This is a special dress, resembling the drab, inconspicuous plumage of the duck, which is only worn for a short period in late summer and early autumn, when, having moulted all their flight-feathers at once, the drakes have temporarily lost the power of flight and have become very defenceless.

The change into "eclipse" dress generally starts in early June and is very rapid indeed, being completed in from three to four weeks. The "eclipse" plumage is then retained for about two months until the drake once again moults back into its breeding dress which it wears till the following summer.

Most of the ducks from the Southern Hemisphere have no "eclipse" dress.

PINIONING

People who keep ornamental waterfowl have found that they cannot risk allowing their birds complete use of their wings, regrettable though this may be. Unless conditions are particularly favourable, the danger of valuable ducks and geese straying away from home is too great.

Young geese are particularly liable to wander away if left free-winged during their first year, but once they are a year or more old they become much more stay-at-home, though there is always a risk that they may stray away and be lost, particularly during prolonged snowy weather.

They must therefore be deprived of the power of flight and this can be achieved in one of two ways, by "feather-clipping" or "pinioning".

"Feather-clipping" involves the shortening with a pair of scissors of all the "primary" flight-feathers on *one* wing only, so that when the bird tries to fly, it is unable to do so, as one wing is shorter than the other and it loses its balance. The "primary" wing-feathers are the hard, pointed feathers, ten in number, farthest away from the body. The "secondary" wing-feathers are the shorter, more-rounded feathers nearer to the body. These should never be cut as when folded they help to keep the bird's body warm and dry.

The drawbacks to "feather-clipping" are two-fold; unless carefully done, the raw edges to the cut feathers are always visible and will spoil the bird's appearance and, secondly, the process has to be repeated every autumn as soon as the new flight-feathers have grown. This can easily be forgotten, with the result that the bird becomes free-winged and is liable to fly away.

As it has to be done only once in a lifetime, pinioning is undoubtedly the most satisfactory way of preventing waterfowl from flying and if properly carried out at an early age causes no suffering at all. Some people like to pinion their ducklings and goslings as soon as they are hatched, when the wings are still very small, but in our opinion the operation should be delayed until the young birds are about three weeks to a month old, by which time their wings have grown a little and one can more easily see what one is doing.

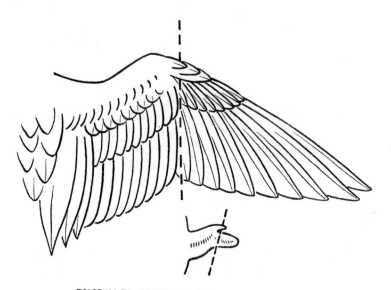

DIAGRAM TO ILLUSTRATE HOW TO PINION A BIRD

Top figure—wing of fully-fledged bird
Bottom figure—wing of young bird before feathers have grown

Dotted line indicates approximate position where wing should be severed. In the case of the fully-fledged bird the cut should be made slightly to the left of the dotted line just beneath the edge of the wing coverts.

The operation is perfectly simple. Holding the bird in the hand, one of its wings should be spread out to its fullest extent when it will be seen that on the forward edge near the tip there is a small protuberance known as the "bastard-wing". This corresponds to the thumb on the human hand. With a pair of very sharp scissors snip off with one clean cut the entire end of the wing from just beyond the "bastard-wing". The duckling will probably be quite unconcerned by the operation and will start to bathe or feed as soon as it is replaced on the ground. If the pinioning has to be delayed till the wing-quills are beginning to sprout, a certain amount of bleeding may take place, but this has no ill effects and at this early age the wound will be completely healed in a few days.

Adult ducks can be pinioned in the same way provided a strong and very sharp pair of scissors are used. By this time of course the "bastard-wing" will be feathered and most of the bird's "primary" flight-feathers will be removed with the piece of severed wing. Owing to the thickness of their wing-bones the pinioning of adult swans and geese should never be carried out except under an anaesthetic by a skilled veterinary surgeon.

A pinioned bird is in no way disfigured and if the operation has been properly carried out, when the wings are folded the lack of the "primary" feathers on one side is scarcely noticeable.

If, for any reason, it is desired to prevent a duck or goose from flying for a few days only, it can, as a very temporary measure, be what is known as "wing-brailed". This consists of fastening one end of a thin strap or piece of strong tape round the "elbow" joint of one wing and then with the wing half-closed, passing the other end of the tape along the outside of the wing, through between the second and third "primary" feathers and back again on the underside of the wing, tying it again round the tape at the "elbow" joint.

This in effect prevents the bird from fully extending one of its wings and so prevents it from flying. The brail must not be kept in place for more than a few days on end or the bird may lose permanently the use of its wing.

Drake Mallard, in full and eclipse plumages.

CHAPTER 7

AILMENTS AND DISEASES

AIM FOR PREVENTION

Generally speaking, ducks and geese are hardy creatures once they have reached maturity and given correct feeding and reasonable care and protection they will live to a considerable age.

The smaller ducks such as Shovelers and Teal can be expected to live at least ten to twelve years and the Shelducks up to twenty, while most species of wild geese live much longer; for them a life-span of twenty-five years is not unusual and there are well-authenticated cases of a Chinese gander at Kew which was known to be over fifty years old and of a wild White-fronted Goose in America which also survived to that age.

Nevertheless, like most living things, waterfowl are subject at times to certain ailments and diseases and the waterfowl-keeper should be able to recognize and treat those that are most likely to occur. If in doubt, he will be well advised to send at once for a veterinary surgeon as it is never wise to assume that a bird is just temporarily "off-colour".

Most ducks and geese will continue to feed until they are practically *in extremis,* so loss of appetite is often one of the last symptoms of illness. For this reason careful watch should be kept on one's birds at all times and particularly when they are being fed, and any bird that seems dull and lethargic or weak on its legs should be caught up and examined at once. Of course dull, lack-lustre plumage is usually a sign of ill-health, but it is quite easy for a bird to "go light" without

42

its plumage showing any obvious signs of illness and a "light" or thin bird is naturally more susceptible to disease than a plump bird.

Although one can usually tell merely by looking at it whether or not a duck or goose is in good condition, it is no bad plan occasionally to catch up a bird here and there from one's flock just to see that all is well. This is one of the many reasons why hand-tameness is so desirable among waterfowl.

Mysterious deaths are liable to occur occasionally in any collection and, if accident can be ruled out, it is always advisable to have the corpse sent away for "post-mortem" examination.

COMMON ILLNESSES

The following are the most usual complaints to which ducks and geese are prone:*

Pneumonia is probably responsible for more "mysterious" deaths among young stock than any other complaint. It is of course most prevalent in cold, wet weather. Unforunately the symptoms are not very noticeable at first and by the time one realizes that the bird is ill, it is often too late for a cure to be likely. The best chance of saving a duckling or gosling which is thought to be suffering from pneumonia is to treat it as though it were a human invalid, keeping it well wrapped up in a warm place and, if it is not too ill to eat, there is a fair chance of its recovery.

Coccidiosis in ducks is rather uncommon, but in geese it is a more frequent cause of death. It is not a quick killer and provided it is recognized and taken in time it can, with modern drugs, be very quickly cured.

The symptoms of a bird suffering from "coccidiosis" vary but generally it loses condition to a marked degree, is feeble on its legs and seems always hungry. Its "droppings" become loose and show traces of blood. Treatment consists in segregating the bird and dosing it for four days running with the drug "sulphamezathine" which can be given either in liquid form in the drinking water or as a powder mixed with the mash. The dose which is usually recommended for a bird the size of a duck is 0.05 grammes per day. For geese the dose should be doubled.

---

* New drugs are constantly being developed and, therefore, readers may find that improved remedies are available.

"Sulphamezathine" should not be given for more than four days running. If it is necessary to give a second treatment, four clear days must be allowed between.

As a preventative a four-day course of the drug can safely be given every six months at the rate of one gramme for every twenty birds and is best given mixed in the morning mash.

Sprawls is a complaint from which growing ducklings and goslings occasionally suffer though we ourselves have had no first-hand experience of it in a life-time of waterfowl-keeping. Opinions differ as to the cause, but it is now generally believed to be due to a vitamin deficiency. The birds, which otherwise appear to be in perfect condition, suddenly lose the power of their legs which stick out sideways from their bodies, while the sufferers have to progress by pushing themselves along the ground on their breasts.

The complaint appears to be curable, but expert advice should be obtained.

Cramp, which has very similar symptoms to the above, affects both adults and young for no apparent reason. One suddenly finds a duck—geese seem less susceptible when adult—lying on the ground quite unable to use its legs and only able to flap along with its wings in the most distressing manner. Twenty-four hours in a box lined with dry straw or hay will generally bring about a complete cure.

Sunstroke. Until they are fully-fledged, young ducklings and goslings sometimes suffer from sunstroke and though they revel in and should be allowed all the sunshine they can get, they must always be provided with some shade in to which they can move if the heat begins to cause them discomfort. On hot summer days, leafy boughs should be spread over part of the coop and run. When suffering from sunstroke ducklings and goslings throw themselves on their backs and will soon die unless they are quickly taken up and moved into a cool, shady spot.

Wet-feather. This is one of the most puzzling and annoying complaints to which waterfowl are liable. It is by no means common. Some collections experience it occasionally, others never. Even the experts do not agree on its cause or cure, but as to its symptoms there is no doubt. The bird loses, either partially or completely, the waterproof qualities of its feathers, so that when out in the rain or when swimming, its plumage becomes soaked and draggled to such an extent that it loses all buoyancy and can easily drown.

44

PLATE 10

Photo : Brian C. Turner

COMMON PINTAIL DRAKE. ONE OF THE EASIEST AND MOST ATTRACTIVE
DUCKS TO KEEP

PLATE 11

Photo : Richard Burn

PINK-FOOTED AND WHITE-FRONTED GEESE IN AN ENCLOSURE PLANTED WITH ORNAMENTAL SHRUBS. NOTE SLIGHT LANDSCAPING WHICH DOES AWAY WITH "FLAT" EFFECT

Waterfowl-keepers have long known that adult salt-water ducks such as Scoters, Goldeneyes and Scaup, if kept away from water for no more than a day or two, tend to lose completely the waterproofing of their feathers and then, if put back onto deep water, their plumage becomes saturated and they can quickly drown. The same thing may happen to hand-reared ducks which have been given no chance to swim or bathe during the fledging period. Though fully-grown and apparently in perfect plumage, we have seen them, when turned out straight onto a pond, become in a few minutes so saturated that they cannot swim and finally, unless rescued in time, they sink to the bottom and drown. It is hard to believe that such a thing could happen to a duck—but it can!

The cause of this complaint is not easy to discover, though one can readily understand that a duckling reared from birth under a hen, must lack much of the natural feather-oil which a mother-duck would naturally transmit to her young from her own plumage. However, one would expect a mature duck, even when hand-reared, to have developed sufficient oil from its own oil-gland to dress its feathers and this is generally the case when ducklings are allowed, from early days, free access to water for swimming and bathing purposes.

We have sometimes noticed that when ducks have been kept on a small pool which has become very foul and sour, or have been penned too closely with others of their kind with resulting soiling of the feathers, they develop "wet-feather" to a greater or lesser extent. But a cure is quickly effected when the ducks can get onto fresh clean water and clean up their feathers.

Geese are very much less prone to "wet-feather" and it is seldom serious, being due generally to over-preening, when for some reason a bird will not leave certain of it feathers alone. The only way to treat a bad case of "wet-feather" is to keep the patient away from water altogether until the natural oils have returned to the feathers. In a mild case the bird should be allowed to remain loose until the next moult, when the new feathers will probably be quite healthy.

Gizzard Worm. This wasting complaint is largely confined to geese and can prove serious for young goslings unless taken in time. It is not at all common. Treatment takes the form of dosing with one of the brands of proprietary drugs sold for the purpose. They are easily administered.

White-Eye sometimes occurs when a large number of ducklings are kept together in a confined space and the complaint is apparently rather contagious. It is undoubtedly caused by over-crowded and dirty conditions.

The symptoms are at first not very noticeable. One or both eyes of the affected bird begin to look watery, with the formation of a cluster of small bubbles at the corner of the eye. Then the whole eye becomes covered with bubbles while the down or feathers round it are caked and messy and finally the eye closes up altogether. The duckling will be constantly scratching and rubbing its eye, which only makes matters worse.

If the complaint is noticed in time it is easily cured. The bird should be isolated and the eye bathed several times a day with cotton wool soaked in some mild disinfectant such as boracic-powder or T.C.P., diulted in warm water. The cure should be complete in a few days.

We have had isolated cases of this ailment due apparently to ducklings getting a small piece of grit or dirt under the eyelid.

Ticks. Very occasionally a young duck or gosling will be found to be suffering from ticks—probably sheep ticks, picked up accidentally from bracken or heather. The ticks affix themselves to the eyelid, ear or base of the bill and can be a nuisance though they seldom prove fatal. They can be persuaded to fall if a dab of paraffin is applied to them. They should never be pulled off by force or the head of the insect is liable to be left behind and cause a sore place.

Aspergillosis is an infection of the respiratory organs caused by a mould. The infective spores are microscopic and are distributed very widely in nature so that most farm workers and farm stock must inhale many every day without apparent harm. Only when a bird is confined on mouldy litter in unhygienic surroundings does it inhale a sufficiently massive dose of mould spores for lesions to develop in the air sacs.

The development of the disease is insidious and usually the only symptom is a gradual loss of condition. Some individuals may show gasping breathing, followed by sudden death. Young birds are the most susceptible and high mortality can occur in individual broods.

Treatment is of no avail; indeed a correct diagnosis is unlikely to be made during life but once a post-mortem reveals *aspergillosis* as the cause of death, immediate steps must be taken to improve conditions under which the waterfowl are being kept.

Salmonellosis. This disease must be mentioned in any chapter on the ailments of waterfowl, because ducks quite commonly carry the infection although few ever suffer from it, and the waterfowl-keeper will be unlucky indeed if ever he meets a case in an adult bird.

Salmonella bacteria are related to the paratyphoid organisms which infect human beings and they are responsible for the bad name which ducks' eggs have earned as a cause of food poisoning. Because they are fairly common in ducks, the finding of these bacteria in the intestines of an adult duck at post mortem is not necessarily evidence of the cause of death.

However, bacteria of this type can cause heavy losses among ducklings of a few days old, particularly when eggs have been hatched in an incubator and one species of Salmonella—*S. typhi murium,* which is commonly carried by rats and mice, may be found to be the cause. Ducklings infected with this complaint show signs of sleepiness, trembling and gasping and sometimes bloody diarrhoea may be seen. In adult birds greenish diarrhoea and listlessness again are suspicious. as is any sudden death.

Treatment of individual cases of *Salmonellosis* is seldom called for, and strict attention to hygiene with elimination of rats and mice should keep the disease away.

CHAPTER 8

SOME WATERFOWL DESCRIBED: OUR NATIVE DUCKS

WIDE VARIETY AVAILABLE

Anyone planning to start a collection of ornamental waterfowl nowadays has a larger variety of species to choose from than ever before. There are now so many enthusiasts in Britain who breed ducks and geese for pleasure and profit that building up a varied collection should present few problems, though prices are high for some species.

Our native British ducks alone include nearly a dozen species of which the drakes can hold their own in any company, and at the present time there is no great dicffiulty in obtaining hand-reared pairs of most of them.

In this chapter we shall give an account of the various kinds of British wild ducks which are suitable for a mixed collection, including their good and bad (if any) qualities, from the point of view of the gardener.

As excellent coloured-plates of all the species mentioned are to be found in most standard works on British birds, we shall confine ourselves to describing only the most striking features of their plumage.

Our native ducks include the following:

THE MALLARD (*Anas platyrhynchos*). This, the commonest of our native ducks, both in captivity and in a wild state, and believed to be the stock from which most domestic species originated, is particularly suitable for the beginner to waterfowl-keeping, being easy to feed and to rear, very hardy, and also very easily tamed.

Mallard look their best in a flock of which some can be left full-winged to fly about if they wish, for they are stay-at-home birds and always remember where food and security is to be had. A friend of ours who lives on the outskirts of a large town, keeps a pair or two of Mallard in his garden. They are quite free-winged and fly off daily to the nearest marshes or river but return regularly at feeding time, winging their way in over the house-tops and alighting with the utmost confidence in their own garden.

Unfortunately, Mallard drakes are of a bullying and masterful nature and cannot be trusted to mix peacefully with other smaller waterfowl during the breeding season, but must be confined in a pen by themselves until mid-summer when they can be released again without danger. Mallards hybridize freely with other species of duck. They are not entirely blameless in the garden but on the whole do not do a great deal of harm and probably do some good in return by eating slugs. The ducklings are easy to feed and to rear. *Incubation period 28 days.*

THE PINTAIL (*Anas acuta*). Nearly as large as the Mallard but slimmer and more elegant, the Pintail drake attracts attention in any company by the beauty of its shape and colouring. It is indeed one of the most graceful of all the ducks, particularly in flight, but unfortunately it is a wanderer and cannot be allowed full use of its wings. Though the drakes fight among themselves at nesting time, they are fairly peaceable with other ducks and completely harmless in the garden.

Hand-reared Pintails breed readily when a year old, but wild-caught birds seldom do so and are not always easy to tame. The nest is placed in rough grass or under a shrub or small conifer, and the first eggs are laid early in April.

The young ducklings are hardy and can be treated much like young Mallard. *Incubation period 23 days.*

THE GADWALL (*Anas strepera*) is one of the rarest as well as the least brightly-clad of all the British surface-feeding ducks. But even so the drake is an attractive bird when in breeding dress with its grey-pencilled back and flanks and black crescent-shaped marks on neck and breast. In spring and summer it has a curious deep croak like a frog.

The female is a smaller and greyer edition of the Mallard duck. Both sexes have a chestnut, black and white wing-mirror instead of the usual blue or green one worn by most of their relatives.

Although the Gadwall occurs in some numbers in eastern England in a wild state, we have not found it very robust in captivity and it seems to lose condition rather quickly in severe weather, for which reason it should be given some protection or extra food during really cold spells. In other respects it is as easy to keep as the Mallard.

The young, which are rather like pale Mallard ducklings, are easy to rear and require the same treament as the latter. *Incubation period 23–24 days.*

THE WIGEON (*Anas penelope*) is really a bird of the sea-shore and river estuary, but large numbers occur inland on lakes and reservoirs during the winter and it seems equally happy on either fresh or salt water. It does well in captivity provided it has plenty of short grazing grass, the shorter the better.

The Wigeon drake in full plumage is a very striking bird with its grey and white body and rich chestnut head. It has a delightful whistle "whee-oo", while the duck, which is a rather dull grey-brown, has a curious growing call.

Wigeon are seen at their best when two or three pairs are kept together, as they are naturally gregarious and quite peaceful with each other and other ducks. If hand-reared they tame easily, but wild-caught birds never become really confiding though they vary individually. They breed quite freely when hand-reared and make good parents.

If allowed free range on a large lawn or paddock, they will be very largely self-supporting during the summer months. Unfortunately they have a great liking for aubretia and dianthus, and these plants should be protected from their attentions during the winter and early spring. When green food is plentiful they leave them alone.

The ducklings are easily reared. *Incubation takes 25 days.*

THE COMMON TEAL (*Anas crecca*). Because of their small size and the brilliance of the drake's plumage, Teal are very much sought-after for collections. They are cheerful, lively little birds and look their best in a small flock, particularly at courtship-time when the males swim eagerly about their mates, with much whistling and bowing. Though perfectly friendly with other ducks, they fight fiercely among themselves at nesting-time and casualties are not unknown. Unfortunately, Teal are not easily tamed and are very liable to panic. Even hand-reared birds which start life exceedingly tame, tend to become rather wary when fledged.

The ideal way to keep Teal is in a wired-in aviary where they are safe from rats and cats and can even be left full-winged.

They are not ready breeders in captivity though some individual ducks do nest quite well and will bring up their own young if left undisturbed. A little more care is needed with the ducklings than in the case of, say, Pintail or Mallard. They thrive on plenty of live food.

It is as well to remember that the nest is often placed a good distance from water. Most of the above remarks would apply equally well to the next species. *Incubation period 23 days.*

THE GARGANEY OF SUMMER TEAL (*Anas querquedula*) is a summer visitor only to this country in a wild state, but in captivity it proves absolutely hardy in the most severe winters. No larger than the Common Teal, it is very similar in habits and even more attractive in appearance with its chocolate poll, broad white eye-stripe and very pale grey flanks. Unfortunately the drake only wears this handsome plumage for a short time as its "eclipse" period lasts from June or July to the following February.

Garganeys are cheerful, sprightly little birds and are more easily tamed than Teal. One of their most attractive features is the curious clicking note of the drakes from which they also get their name of "Cricket Teal". The ducks have a rather sad little quack. They are shy breeders and the young are delicate.

Both Garganey and Teal are entirely harmless in the garden. *Incubation period 23 days.*

THE SHOVELER (*Spatula clypeata*). One of the most brightly-clad and attractive of all our wild-fowl, the Shoveler is worthy of a place in the most select collection. It is in many ways rather a clown with its huge spoon-shaped bill, very small feet and croaking quack, but it is also a bird of character and is easily tamed.

It breeds freely in captivity and if its eggs are taken the duck will lay a second or even a third clutch in a season. Unfortunately the ducklings often prove difficult to rear, being very liable to catch cold, and they require a great deal of insect food during the first few weeks.

Shovelers are more insectivorous than most of the ducks, and in hard weather they will benefit from extra feeding as they lose condition quickly. They are, like all ducks, real gluttons for worms and we well remember one of our particular tame broods which always attended the gardener whenever they saw him digging the flower beds. *Incubation pediod 23 days.*

All the ducks we have mentioned so far are what are known as "surface-feeding" or "dabbling" ducks, that is to say they obtain most of their food on dry land or from bogs or shallow water where they only need to put their heads and necks below the surface to reach it. They seldom, or never, dive for their food.

The next two species are known as "diving-ducks" because they obtain their food—insects and water plants—almost entirely by diving in deep water, sometimes as deep as six to ten feet. In captivity they are easily tamed, and come ashore quite readily to eat corn or bread or mash.

In a natural pond the diving-ducks are rather liable to stir up the mud as they forage for food on the bottom, but this trouble does not arise when they are kept in a concrete pool. They are quite harmless in the garden and will be found most excellent for clearing off surplus water-weed from moat or lake.

TUFTED DUCK (*Aythya fuligula*). This is the small black and white duck with the crest and the yellow eyes, which is so plentiful on the lakes in our London parks, where its tameness and antics when diving for bread make it very popular with the public.

The Tufted Duck walks easily, if inelegantly, on dry land where it looks, with its upright carriage and black and white plumage, rather like a small penguin. It should be included in all collections.

It breeds rather uncertainly in captivity and nests later than most ducks, eggs seldom being laid before late May. They are grey-green and very large for the size of the bird. The nest is usually built in rushes near to, or actually over water, though not always. The ducklings are not easy to rear as they require a great deal of animal food, particularly water-snails, to start with, but at the age of about a month they will usually take to a diet of pellets, mash, etc. *Incubation period 25–26 days.*

COMMON POCHARD (*Aythya ferina*). Though it lacks some of the popular appeal of the Tufted Duck, the Common Pochard is an asset to any collection. Particularly in summertime, against a background of green reeds, the drake's bright chestnut head, red eye and lavender-grey body are most striking and the bird has a pleasant little wheezing call. Hand-reared Pochard become very tame indeed, but wild-caught birds are never satisfactory. The nest is always built in a clump of rushes actually over the water. The eggs are greenish and rather large for the size of the bird. Pochards breed moderately freely in captivity. The ducklings are hardy and robust and are not difficult to rear if started on a diet of insects and worms. *Incubation period 25 days.*

THE SCAUP *(Aythya marila)* is the only salt-water duck which we consider really suitable for the small collection. It is also a diving-duck, and in a wild state inhabits rocky coasts and scaup-beds—hence its name—but when hand-reared it becomes perfectly adapted to a life on fresh water. The drake is an ornamental bird with a glossy, bluegreen head, black breast, white underparts, and grey back, while the duck is brown with a white band at the base of the bill. In captivity the Scaup does quite well on a normal diet of mash and corn, but should be provided occasionally with cod-liver oil or fish meal in its mash. It does not breed freely in captivity. *Incubation period 28 days.*

OTHER POSSIBILITIES

The remaining "sea ducks", that is to say the Eider, the Long-tailed Duck, the Goldeneye, the Barrow's Goldeneye and the Scoters, are not recommended for anyone just starting a collection as they call for rather special treatment. To start with, their diet must contain a percentage of cod-liver oil, fish meal, boiled liver, boiled rabbit, shrimps, etc., in fact, a very much more "meaty" diet than most ducks require. This food should be given mixed in a daily mash and to ensure that the other ducks which do not need such rich fare cannot get at it, in a mixed collection, the "sea ducks" will have, somehow, to be fed separately. Where Eider Ducks are concerned this presents no difficulty as they become embarrassingly tame and will take all their food from the hand, but some of the other salt-water ducks do not tame so easily.

However, they are all interesting birds and some at least are highly ornamental.

CHAPTER 9

MORE WATERFOWL DESCRIBED:

THE EXOTIC DUCKS

When we come to the exotic ducks—birds from such places as India and Australia, Africa and South America—we find ourselves faced with a bewildering variety to choose from, many of them most striking and beautiful in appearance.

Unfortunately a number which, before the war, were quite plentiful in collections, have now become scarce and owing to import restrictions, stocks in this country can only be increased again by home-bred birds. Some kinds are accordingly still expensive and difficult to acquire.

But the position is improving every year and it should not be long before all but the very rarest waterfowl are obtainable in fair numbers.

Although there are at the present time stocks of between thirty or forty kinds of "foreign" duck in collections in this country, we have thought it advisable to confine ourselves in this chapter to a description of a dozen or so of what we consider to be the most suitable kinds for a small collection from the point of view of beauty, hardiness and ease of acquisition.

MAIN SPECIES

The species which we particularly recommend are as follows:

THE MANDARIN (*Aix galericulata*), by common consent, heads the list both for beauty of colouring and charm of habits. A small duck, midway in size between the Teal and the Wigeon, it is a native of eastern Asia, including Japan, but within recent years has become well established in a wild state in several parts of this country, particularly in Surrey.

Words cannot do full justice to the beauty of the Mandarin drake in full plumage. A mixture of chestnut and buff, purple and blue, boldly slashed with black and white, it has a chestnut and green crest, long "dundreary whiskers", and two wonderful fan-shaped feathers which stand erect like sails above its back. The duck somewhat resembles a pigeon in shape and colouring, for it is blue-grey with light mottling on flanks and shoulders, white spectacles round the eyes, and blue and grey wings (*see frontispiece*).

At all times active and lively, Mandarins are seen at their best during their courtship display which involves a most elaborate ceremonial with much running to and fro, with bowing of heads and raising of crests, while on the water the drakes swim busily about their mates like little full-rigged ships in sail.

In a wild state Mandarins nest in holes in trees, but in confinement they take readily to nesting boxes placed a few feet from the ground in shrubs or trees, and provided with a suitable branch to act as a ladder for getting up and down to the nest. Hollow logs or drainpipes with a suitable nesting cavity, are also popular. The eggs, which are laid in late April or May, are pinkish and highly glossed.

We have not found Mandarins particularly free breeders and they seldom lay fertile eggs till their second year. The ducklings, which are most intelligent little creatures, are hardy and not difficult to rear. With a little encouragement they become very tame.

Paired Mandarins are most devoted to each other and quite harmless to other waterfowl, and to garden plants. They have been kept free-winged quite successfully on some large estates, notably at Woburn Abbey and at Foxwarren Park in Surrey, where they apparently did not wander a great deal, but on a small garden pond we should consider it highly risky to leave both birds of a pair completely free-winged.

The "eclipse" period is short, extending from June to August, and the young drake assumes full plumage in its first autumn. Before this it can be distinguished from the young duck by its slightly reddish bill and by the black and white stripes on the side of its breast which are the first traces of its adult plumage to appear. *Incubation period 30 days.*

57

THE CAROLINA *(Aix sponsa)* or WOOD DUCK, a native of North America, is closely related to the Mandarin, which it resembles in habits and general pattern of plumage. Opinions differ as to which of the two is the more beautiful. The Carolina is perhaps the less striking, as it lacks the wing-fans and bright reds and buffs of the Mandarin. Instead it is a study in purple, green, blue and olive, with a brilliant red eye, a red and orange bill, and a long, drooping crest *(see plate 14)*.

Mandarin and Carolina ducks are very similar indeed in appearance, but the female Carolina usually has more white round the eyes. The young drake Carolinas can be distinguished from the ducks as soon as fledged, by the double white line which runs from the centre of the cheeks round under the chin.

Once paired, Carolinas remain most devoted to each other, and are seldom seen apart. In nesting habits they resemble Mandarins, but they breed much more readily, laying fertile eggs when a year old. If their eggs are taken, they will often make two or three attempts to nest in a season and will lay as many as thirty eggs, starting in mid-March. The ducklings are nervous and wild when first hatched, and care must be taken to see that they do not escape from the coop or run, for they are great climbers at that age. They are not always easy to rear.

Unfortunately we cannot say that this species is completely harmless in the garden, as early in the year, when green food is scarce, they have a weakness for such plants as aubretia, mecanopsis, Shirley-poppies, etc., but their beauty and charm more than compensates for such small damage as they do. *Incubation period 28–30 days.*

THE AUSTRALIAN WOOD DUCK OR MANED GOOSE *(Chenonetta jubata)*. Closely allied to the two previous species, though it differs from them somewhat in habits, the Maned Goose as it is generally called, is a good deal larger and less brightly coloured. Nonetheless it is an attractive bird, the male having a dark chocolate brown head with a slight crest, a pale grey body and breast heavily spotted with black. The female has a paler head with white streaks above and below the eye and flanks mottled with white. The bill is black, feet and legs grey.

It is gentle and tame and quite hardy. It nests in hollow trees in a wild state, so it should be provided with wooden nest-boxes. *Incubation period 28 days.*

THE BAHAMA PINTAIL (*Anas bahamensis*) comes from South America and the West Indies and, like most of the ducks from the Southern Hemisphere, the sexes are very much alike and there is no "eclipse" dress.

It is particularly popular with waterfowl-keepers, as it is a gentle little bird with pleasing ways and attractive plumage, and proves completely hardy in our climate.

No more than half the size of the Common Pintail, the Bahama is of a general pinkish-brown colour, mottled with dark brown on back and flanks, and with pale, elongated tail feathers. The cheeks are pure white, and the beak bright blue and red. The wing-mirror is a vivid green and buff, and the eye red (*see frontispiece*).

There is also a very attractive mutation sometimes referred to as the White Bahama or the Silver Bahama which is in fact a delicate silver-grey all over but with the normal blue and red bill.

This species does not breed very freely in confinement, and we have found it nervous when nesting, easily deserting its eggs if frightened. The nest is placed on the ground usually against a tree, or at the bottom of a hedge. The eggs, which are pinkish, are laid in May or June. The ducklings are quite hardy but rather timid, and do best when kept apart from other ducklings. The courtship display is charming. *Incubation period 25 days.*

THE CHILOE WIGEON (*Anas sibilatrix*) is another South American duck, and again the sexes are similar, and there is no "eclipse" plumage.

A typical Wigeon in shape and habits, the Chiloë—pronounced "Che-lo-ey"—catches the eye in any company. The general colouring is creamy-white, slashed with black and with an orange wash on the flanks. The head and neck are dark, glossy green, and the bill blueish. The bird is about the size of the Common Wigeon (*see frontispiece*).

The Chiloë Wigeon nests on the ground in thick cover, and the eggs are laid in early May. The young, which require plenty of green food, are not difficult to rear. When adult, the birds are hardy and very tame. Paired birds are at all times devoted, seldom going far from each other and constantly nibbling each other's bills while they indulge in low chattering calls. *Incubation period 25 days.*

THE RED-CRESTED POCHARD (*Netta rufina*) is on the British list, but it is a very rare bird here in a wild state, being found mainly in southern Europe and Asia, as far east as India.

This is a most desirable duck for any collection, being handsome, tame and hardy. The drake is a striking bird, the feathers of its head being long and silky and of a rich golden chestnut hue. The bill and feet are red, and the eye vivid orange-red. The breast and underparts are glossy black, divided from the brown back by a band of pinkish white. The female is brown, with grey streaks and underparts, and a pinkish bill.

Like most diving-ducks, the Red-crested Pochard is a greedy bird, and very soon becomes very tame. It is very fond of waterweed and is a great grazer, but quite harmless in the garden. It frequently breeds when a year old, making a large and rather elaborate nest, sometimes quite a long way from water. Eggs are laid early in April.

The ducklings, which resemble Mallards in colouring except for their pink beaks, are hardy and easily reared. The young drakes, when first hatched, are distinguishable from the ducks by the greater brightness of their beaks, and when fledged, they always have pinker beaks and feet, and lighter-coloured eyes. *Incubation period 25 days.*

THE ROSYBILL (*Netta peposaca*), a South American duck, belongs to the Pochard family. It is a large bird and appears rather clumsy and ungainly on land, but is very ornamental on the water. The drake is glossy-black on head, back and breast, with grey-pencilled flanks, red eyes and a vivid rose-pink bill. The female is dull brown and there is no "eclipse".

Although the Rosybill proves quite hardy in this country, it does not breed freely unless conditions suit its taste. It likes to nest in tall herbage, close to, or over water, where it makes a large, untidy structure, typical of the Pochards. The eggs are large and are laid in early May. The young are easy to rear, but require an abundance of water-weed. The young drakes develop a pinkish tinge to the bill early in life. The adults are friendly with other waterfowl and quite harmless in the garden. *Incubation period 25–26 days.*

THE CHILEAN TEAL (*Anas flavirostris*) also comes from South America. It is popular in collections, as it is a friendly and gentle little duck and quite ornamental. Slightly larger than the Common Teal, it is a soft greyish-fawn colour, mottled with dark brown, and has a green and black wing-mirror. The bill is bright yellow, with a black streak down the centre. The female is similar, though her colourings are less bright. Quite harmless in the garden.

In the natural state, Chilean Teal breed in trees, but in confinement they nest readily in tall grass or other low cover as well as in hollow logs. The young are not difficult to rear if given a certain amount of insect food to start with. The adult drake has a clear short whistle. *Incubation period 25–26 days.*

THE CINNAMON TEAL (*Anas cyanoptera*) is a native of North and South America. About the same size as the Common Teal, but with a longer bill, it is a very handsome species indeed. The drake is a rich, cinnamon-red, with bright-blue shoulders, a green wing-mirror, a red eye and a black bill. The duck is much like the female Common Teal, but rather paler. Although called a Teal, the Cinnamon is really more closely related to the Shovelers, which it resembles in general habits. In "eclipse" plumage the drake takes after his mate, but he retains the blue shoulders. The nest is like that of other Teal and is well hidden in thick grass and undergrowth. The young should be treated like young Shovelers and protected from wet and cold.

Gentle with other ducks and quite harmless in the garden. *Incubation period 23 days.*

THE CHESTNUT-BREASTED TEAL (*Anas castanea*) comes from Australia. This is one of the few ducks from the Southern Hemisphere in which the sexes are dissimilar. The drake has a dark, glossy-green head and neck, red eyes, and breast and flanks chestnut mottled with black. It is about the size of the Bahama Pintail. The female is brown, with dark mottlings. Both sexes have blue bills and legs.

They are lively and attractive birds, with habits rather resembling those of the Carolina and Mandarin, and they readily make use of the nesting-boxes provided for the latter birds.

The Chestnut-breasted Teal is not, unfortunately, a very free nester in captivity, though the young are hardy enough and quite easy to rear. Quite harmless to other waterfowl and in the garden. *Incubation pediod 27 days.*

THE SPOTBILL (*Anas poecilorhyncha*) is an Asiatic duck with a number of races, all rather similar in appearance.

Opinions may differ as to the value of this species in a collection, but in our view it is a handsome and desirable duck.

The Spotbill belongs to the Mallard family and is slightly larger than the drake Mallard. The sexes are very much alike. They are greyish-white, mottled with black, and have a black tail. The wing-mirror is brilliant green and white. The bill is black, with a bright yellow tip, and a small patch of red or orange at the base. The feet and legs are brilliant orange-red. There is no "eclipse" dress.

In general habits the Spotbills resemble Mallards, nesting in low cover and rearing their young quite successfully. They stand our climate well and are not destructive in the garden, though, like Mallard, they will occasionally graze down a succulent green plant when grass is scarce in the early spring. *Incubation period 26 days.*

THE FALCATED TEAL (*Anas falcata*) comes from Eastern Asia. Although not one of the cheaper ducks to purchase at the present time, it is so very unusual in appearance that every effort should be made to obtain a pair for the collection. The drake has a shaggy crest of a beautiful coppery-green colour, black and white chin and throat, and grey-pencilled flanks. Its chief adornment, however, are the long, sickle-shaped wing feathers, which curve right over the tail, almost concealing it from view. The duck is dull brown, rather like a Gadwall in appearance, but with a darker bill. In "eclipse" the drake resembles his mate, but is slightly darker.

Apart from their appearance, which is most striking, Falcated Teal are rather dull and sluggish birds, but they are perfectly hardy, and harmless in the garden, and with other waterfowl. They breed freely in confinement, nesting in thick grass and shrubs, and the young are easily reared.

The drake has a delightful whistling call. *Incubation takes 26 days.*

THE BRAZILIAN TEAL (*Amazonetta brasiliensis*). Inhabits South America. A rather small brownish grey surface-feeding duck, its chief characteristic being the colour of its feet and legs which are a most brilliant cornelian red. The drake also has a red bill, while that of the duck is grey.

This duck makes an attractive and worthy addition to any collection, particularly as it is always in colour. *Incubation period 25 days.*

THE ARGENTINE RED SHOVELER (*Anas platalea*). This is the most highly coloured of the shovelers, having a light grey head, reddish-chestnut body plumage heavily spotted with darker brown, a white eye and a black bill. The female is somewhat like the European Shoveler. They are very similar to the latter in habits and disposition. *Incubation period 23 days.*

THE CAPE TEAL (*Anas capensis*). This ornamental and attractive duck is about the size of a Mandarin. The sexes are alike, being of a greyish colour, spotted and barred with brown. They have

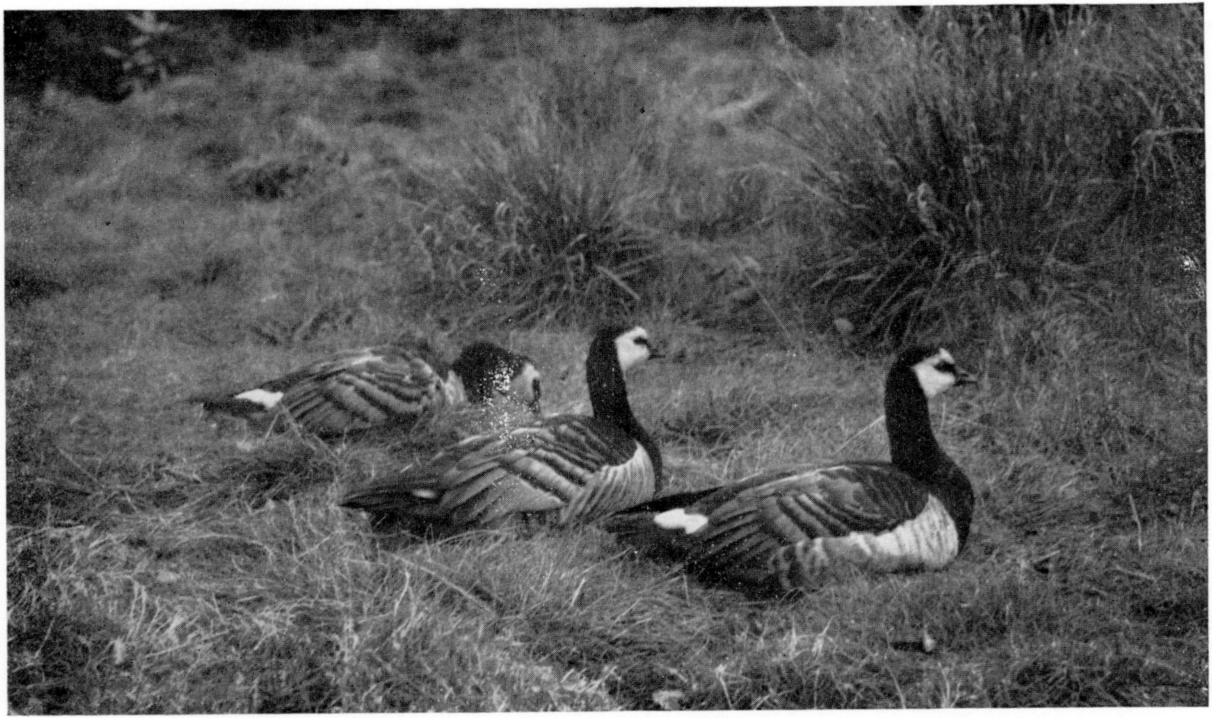

PLATE 12

BARNACLE GEESE

63

PLATE 13

Photo : Pamela Harrison

TRANQUILITY - MALE AND FEMALE GADWALL

pink eyes and an upturned bluish-pink bill and a green, black and white wing-mirror. They are talkative birds and a trifle domineering but we have not found them difficult to keep with other smaller species. They are always in colour and are quite hardy. *Incubation period 25–26 days.*

THE BLUE-WINGED TEAL (*Anas discors*). An American species about the size of the European Teal, it has a rather longer bill and is nearer to the shovelers. The drake is very handsome when in full plumage, having a body colour of dark grey, speckled with light and dark brown, a purple-grey head with a crescent-shaped white mark on the face and brilliant sky-blue shoulders. The feet are yellow. The female is rather similar to the Common Teal but has the blue shoulders of the male. They are quiet and friendly with other waterfowl. *Incubation period 23 days.*

THE BAIKAL TEAL (*Anas formosa*) is one of the real gems of the duck world and deserves a place in any collection. It is some-what larger than a Common Teal. The drake has a glossy black crown and chin, while the creamy buff cheeks are slashed by a black streak running down from the eye and by a broad green band running backwards to the nape. The finely pencilled flanks are slate blue, the scapulars chestnut, black and cream. The wing-mirror is white, black, green and cinnamon. The bill and legs are grey (*see foot of page*).

The female is very like that of the Common Teal in appearance but has a small white patch as the base of the bill and a white chin and throat.

Owing to its scarcity the Baikal Teal is still rather an expensive bird to buy and most of those on offer in Britain at present are imported wild-caught birds. However a hand-reared stock is gradually being built up.

This teal breeds in Eastern Siberia and winters in China and Japan. *Incubation period 23–25 days.*

THE LAYSAN TEAL (*Anas platyrhynchos laysanensis*). If a really tame species is required there is none better than this duck which originates on the small island of Laysan in the Pacific. It is a wonderful example of the effectiveness of conservation for some fifty years ago there were reported to be no more than seven individuals left alive on their native island. Yet, now, thanks to protection and to breeding in captivity the Laysan Teal is quite an abundant bird in collections.

Somewhat larger than a Common Teal, it is quite pleasing in appearance, beings a light mottled brown with a good deal of white round the eyes and with a black, white and green wing-mirror.

It breeds very freely, is quite hardy and as already mentioned is ridiculously confiding. *Incubation period 25 days.*

CHAPTER 10

THE SHELDUCKS

SEPARATION ADVISABLE

The Shelduck group is a most interesting one, coming between the Shelgeese and the true ducks and having some of the characteristics of each. Its members are long-legged and spend much of their time on dry land. They are all striking in appearance, with a more or less upright carriage and handsome colouring. They are great grazers.

Shelducks do extremely well in captivity, being very hardy, and often live to an advanced age. In the wild state they breed when two years old and when once they start to lay in confinement, they will do so with regularity, usually producing large clutches of eggs. They nest in holes in trees or rocks or in rabbit burrows and in captivity similar sites should be provided for them and they will readily make use of large nesting boxes with holes cut in the side or small barrels let into the ground.

Unfortunately Shelducks are inclined to be quarrelsome and aggressive, though in this respect the degree varies considerably not only within the species but with individuals. But then we might say the same about individual members of the human species, including the co-authors of this book.

As a result of this aggressiveness it is advisable to keep most of the Shelducks separate from other ducks and geese except where there is a great deal of space. They do not as a rule interfere with swans or small ducks such as Teal but even so it is unwise to include Shelducks in any mixed collection where space is limited. They require very little swimming water, so may be kept in an orchard or small paddock with only a small artificial pool of some sort.

The young of all Shelduck are much alike, being black and white or grey and white, like young Egyptian Geese. They are not difficult to rear and are very hardy.

PRINCIPAL SPECIES

The principal species available are as follows:

THE COMMON SHELDUCK (*Tadorna tadorna*) is a handsome bird, having white body-feathers with a broad chestnut band across the breast and shoulders, a glossy black head and neck, a red bill and pink legs. The female is smaller and lacks the red knob on the bill which the male acquires during the breeding season. The young ducklings are charming and amusing.

At the present time the Common Shelduck is a plentiful and characteristic bird of our British coastal mudflats and sandy estuaries, and is to be found in most public and private collections. In our experience it is not dangerous to other ducks except in a very confined space and we consider it a cheap and attractive addition to any collection.

THE RUDDY SHELDUCK (*Tadorna ferruginea*) as its name suggests, has a rich, coppery-red body, a pale buff head, black tail, legs and bill and black and white wings. These colours show up most strikingly against a green lawn or paddock. Male and female are similar in colouring though the latter is smaller and has more white on the head. There is no actual "eclipse" dress but in spring the drake assumes an indistinct black collar.

They vary a good deal in the intensity of their colouring and strangely enough it sometimes happens that ducklings which have the palest down when young become the most richly coloured when adult.

Their reputation for being quarrelsome with other waterfowl seems undeserved provided they are given plenty of space. Like many of their group, they are bold birds and make excellent watchdogs, their loud braying honk giving immediate warning if any stranger, whether human, canine or feline, appears on the scene. Those who have shot duck in India and neighbouring countries will be well aware of this propensity and will remember with sorrow the occasions when a lengthy stalk has so often been spoiled by the alarm notes of the Brahminy or Ruddy Shelduck. At such times they may well have wondered whether the Ruddy was really named because of its colouring.

THE SOUTH AFRICAN SHELDUCK (*Tadorna cana*) is very similar in appearance to the previous species, the chief difference being that the male has an ashy-grey head while the body plumage of both sexes is rather greyer. They are very quarrelsome but make up for it by being much more ready to breed in captivity. They are very hardy and are well suited to a large lake alongside swans or in an enclosure by themselves.

THE AUSTRALIAN SHELDUCK (*Tadorna tadornoides*) is another handsome species, larger than any of the others and much darker in general appearance. Head and neck are metallic black, breast and mantle cinnamon, with—in the case of the male—a broad white ring round the neck. The female has a narrower white ring round the neck and usually has some white round the eyes. Altogether an attractive-looking bird.

Although by far the largest of the group, Australian Shelducks are, in our experience, by no means the most aggressive, though opinions differ in this respect. We would class them as one of the most desirable, not only in appearance but also in behaviour and would have no hesitation in including them in a mixed collection where there is plenty of space.

At one time these Shelducks were regarded as shy breeders in confinement but now that hand-reared stock is obtainable it should be possible to purchase unrelated pairs which will produce fertile eggs. And once they start to lay they may produce two clutches a year, with a high percentage of fertility and hatchability.

THE PARADISE DUCK OR NEW ZEALAND SHELDUCK (*Tadorna variegata*) is the only other member of the group which we shall mention, though there are a few others which are seldom found in collections. This Shelduck is another large, handsomely-marked bird, though rather smaller than the Australian species which it resembles somewhat in appearance. The male lacks the cinnamon breast and mantle while the female has a pure white head and neck. Unfortunately they are the most savage of all the Shelducks though they can be kept on a large stretch of water with swans and geese. They probably do best in an enclosure by themselves.

Neither the Australian nor the New Zealand Shelducks are particularly plentiful in captivity at the present time, but anyone anxious to obtain a pair should have no great difficulty in doing so. *All have an incubation period of between 28–30 days.*

CHAPTER 11

THE GEESE

GEESE THRIVE ON GRASS

There are a large number of different kinds of wild geese from all parts of the world, and most of them do extremely well in confinement. All they require for good health is plenty of fine, short grass for grazing. Water is only of secondary importance, though some swimming water is usually necessary if the birds are to breed.

A mixed flock of wild geese in a paddock or orchard looks delightful and will give endless pleasure and interest to their owner. Most geese are hardy, long-lived, and intelligent, and many of them are highly ornamental. When hand-reared they often become as tame as dogs, for they all, even wild-caught birds, seem to enjoy human company.

Most of the geese can be kept together even in the breeding season, though some of the South American geese are quarrelsome and spiteful with other species and are better kept separate. The larger races of the Canada Goose should also be kept on their own during the nesting season when the ganders are often very savage.

Because of their size, geese run few risks from vermin, and where foxes are unlikely to be troublesome, can be allowed completely free range in a park or large meadow. For this reason they are recommended for anyone who finds conditions too difficult for keeping the smaller, and more delicate waterfowl.

Some of the smaller kinds of geese, such as the Barnacle, Ross's, Lesser White-fronted, Red-breasted, and the South American geese, can well be kept at liberty in a large garden, provided one's neighbours are unlikely to be disturbed by the birds' calls which can, during the breeding season, be rather penetrating at times.

All geese are great grazers and, provided they have plenty of short grass, they will do little or no damage to garden plants and shrubs. But it is most important to remember that geese will NOT eat long coarse grass; they must have it not more than about three inches long, and the shorter and finer it is the better they like it. Should it become too long and rank, there is nothing for it but to resort to the scythe or mowing-machine, but it is usually not difficult to work out a system where, by alternately grazing and resting different parts of the enclosure or paddock, the birds themselves will keep the grass at the required length.

BREEDING MAY BE DIFFICULT

Unfortunately many of the geese do *not* breed very freely in confinement, and wild-caught birds will sometimes take as much as twenty years before they think of nesting. Even hand-reared birds seldom lay fertile eggs before their third year, and lone pairs seem less ready to breed than when a flock of the same species are kept together. This is not surprising, as many geese nest in colonies in a wild state.

Provided adequate space is available, many different kinds of geese can safely be kept together, particularly those known as the "grey" and "black" geese from the Northern Hemisphere. Certainly the larger and stronger may dominate the smaller species, but only to a minor degree, and fighting and bullying seldom take place. But this is not the case with most of the South American species, the ganders of which are particularly quarrelsome, and in the breeding season really savage, not only with each other, but with other kinds of geese and ducks. It is almost essential to keep pairs of South American geese in pens by themselves or there is a grave risk of the ganders killing or maiming other waterfowl.

The sexes of practically all the geese from the Northern Hemisphere are very much alike, and in the case of the "grey" geese, it requires a most expert eye to distinguish the ganders from the geese. In general the ganders are slightly larger and have thicker and coarser heads and bills, and the "grooves" in the feathers of the neck are more pronounced. The voices of the ganders are also more high-pitched, while the behaviour of the sexes is usually different, the ganders being bold and aggressive with human beings and dogs, while the geese tend to keep themselves in the background.

A CAROLINA DRAKE *Photo : Richard Burn*

Photo : Pamela Harrison
CONTRAST IN STYLE: A NATIVE TUFTED DRAKE

PLATE 14

73

PLATE 15

Photo : Richard Burn

ALL SHELDUCKLINGS DISPLAY THIS CHARACTERISTIC PIED PLUMAGE

74

PLATE 16

Photo : Richard Burn

A GROUP OF SHELDUCKS : COMMON, RUDDY, SOUTH AFRICAN AND AUSTRALIAN

PLATE 17

Photo : Christina Sanday

A GROUP OF RED-BREASTED AND ROSS'S GEESE

NO SPECIAL FEEDING

Wild geese are very easy to keep in good health. They should be given one good meal a day of grain, which can be fed broadcast or in troughs, and in mid-winter, when grass is scarce or frosted or buried beneath the snow, they will eat with relish chopped cabbage or lettuce, or sugar-beet, and at all times of the year they will appreciate household scraps, windfall apples and many juicy weeds such as thistles and poppies and, of course, potatoes.

Most geese can be relied upon to hatch and rear their own young. Both parents are devoted in the care of their goslings, their one fault being a proneness to go off with the first few goslings to be hatched, leaving chipped eggs in the nest. The goslings will start grazing almost as soon as hatched, and they take readily to chopped lettuce, biscuit-meal, mash, etc.

SPECIES OF GEESE

Possible geese for including in a waterfowl collection are as follows:

Among the "grey" geese, all of which occur in Britain as winter visitors, the GREYLAG (*Anser anser*) is the only species which actually breeds in this country, a small number nesting in northern Scotland and the Hebrides.

This goose, the stock from which all of our domestic breeds of geese except the Chinese goose are said to have developed, is in fact a smaller and less clumsy edition of the ordinary Toulouse goose. Its call notes are exactly similar. It is intelligent and easily tamed but otherwise has little to commend it, being a rather coarse-looking, soberly-clad bird compared with some other species.

Greylags nest freely in captivity, the eggs being laid in early April. *Incubation period 27–30 days.*

THE BEAN GOOSE (*Anser fabalis*) is a comparatively scarce winter visitor to this country. It breeds in Lapland and north Russia. It is a large bird, slightly larger than the Greylag, and with a longer, thinner neck. It is easily distinguished by the colouring of the feet which are orange, and of the bill which is black with an orange band, whereas the Greylag has pink feet and a yellowish bill with a white nail.

Though the Bean Goose can hardly be called handsome, it is an interesting bird with a curious and distinctive call and tames very easily. Where space allows, it is worthy of a place in the collection. It does not nest very freely in confinement. *Incubation period 27–30 days.*

THE PINK-FOOTED GOOSE (*Anser brachyrhynchus*) is the commonest of the "grey" geese to visit this country, occurring in considerable numbers in winter in eastern Scotland, the Solway, Yorkshire and Lincolnshire, and in smaller numbers elsewhere.

One of the most elegant and attractive of the grey geese, the Pink-foot is smaller than the Greylag, has a greyish body, chocolate brown neck, pink legs and feet, and a very small, black bill with a pink band. This goose is at present classified by some systematists as being a race of the Bean Goose, but anyone who is well acquainted with it, both in the wild and in confinement, may well find it hard to accept this view.

The Pink-footed Goose does well in confinement and deserves a place in any collection, even though it does not tame as easily as most of the other grey geese.

Up to fifteen years ago most of the Pink-footed geese in captivity were wild caught and therefore non-breeders but since then a good stock of hand-reared and free-breeding birds has been built up in collections.

In captivity the Pink-footed Goose seems to nest earlier than it does in its wild breeding quarters in Greenland and Iceland, first eggs being laid about mid-April.

It is more silent than most geese, but the gander has a delightful high-pitched "pink-quink", rather like the yapping of a small dog, while the goose has a gruffer note. *Incubation period 25–28 days.*

THE WHITE-FRONTED GOOSE (*Anser albifrons*). Two races of this goose visit Britain in winter; one, which has a pink bill and orange legs, occurs on our east and south coast and by the River Severn, while the race from Greenland, which is a darker bird with orange bill and legs, occurs in Ireland and western Scotland.

The White-front is in every way a most attractive bird, with its dark brown plumage, black barred breast, and conspicuous white forehead. It is the same size as the Pink-foot. Less wary in the wild, it is very easily tamed in confinement, and hand-reared birds breed quite freely.

It is a noisy bird with a delightfully musical call, from which it gets its very appropriate name of "Laughing-Goose". Its conversational note is a definite chuckle. *Incubation period 28–30 days.*

THE LESSER WHITE-FRONTED GOOSE *(Anser erythropus).* This very beautiful little goose, which breeds in Lapland and North Russia, is only a rare visitor to Britain in winter. At present it is still comparatively scarce in collections and commands a higher price than those geese already described. Smaller than the common White-front which it resembles in general colouring, it is easily distinguished by its small pink bill, conspicuous yellow eyelids and broad white forehead.

Because of its small size and gentle disposition it is particularly sutable for keeping in a small garden or enclosure. *Incubation period 25–28 days.*

THE GREATER SNOW GOOSE *(Anser caerulescens atlanticus),* THE LESSER SNOW GOOSE *(A. c. hyperboreus),* ROSS'S GOOSE *(Anser rossii).* The Snow Geese breed in Northern Canada or Greenland, migrating to the southern United States in winter. When adult most of them are white with black wings and pink or grey bills. Immature birds are greyer and have dull grey bills. The Lesser Snow goose is dimorphic, having a blue-grey phase sometimes called the Blue Goose, as well as the normal white form. Ross's Goose is the smallest and most attractive, being little larger than a mallard, with black primaries and a very small pink bill. It breeds well in confinement.

All the Snow Geese are hardy and fairly harmless with other waterfowl. *Incubation period 24–28 days.*

THE EMPEROR GOOSE *(Anser canagicus).* This very handsome goose, which hails from Alaska, deserves a place in any collection. It is silvery-grey, heavily barred with black and white. The head and hind neck are white, set off by a black chin and throat. The bill is pinkish blue, the feet and legs deep yellow. Immature birds are duller. The Emperor Goose is quiet and easily tamed and is a great grazer. *Incubation period 26–28 days.*

THE BAR-HEADED GOOSE *(Anser indicus)* breeds in central Asia and winters in India. It is a medium-sized goose, of which the general colour is light grey, barred with white, and with yellow bill and legs. The head and cheeks are white and this colour extends down the side of the neck as far as the shoulders. The rest of the neck is black, and there are two broad black bars across the top of the head. First-year birds have dark brown and white heads without the black bars.

A popular bird in collections, the Bar-headed Goose is completely hardy and breeds freely from the age of three years. It is good tempered with other waterfowl, and has the great merit that, once well established in suitable surroundings, it shows little inclination to wander away and can usually be left full-winged. The young should be wing-clipped for the first year. *Incubation period 28–30 days.*

THE CANADA GOOSE (*Branta canadensis*) is now established as a wild breeding-bird in many parts of Britain, though it is in fact a native of North America.

This large and very handsome goose should be included in any mixed collection where adequate space is available. It needs, or rather likes, more swimming space than most of its relatives, and spends a great deal of time on the water. Where suitable conditions exist, such as a large park with a lake, Canada Geese should be allowed full use of their wings for they seldom wander far from their home waters and they look particularly attractive in flight.

The Canada Goose has a glossy black head and neck, with a conspicuous white cheek patch, a pale breast and undeparts, and ash-brown body. The tail is black and there is a white band across the rump. Though not in any way shy, it seldom becomes as tame and friendly as other geese and it seems to be one of the least intelligent.

Given plenty of space, it breeds freely from its third year, and is a good parent. The nest is usually placed close to water, an island being a favourite site, and first eggs are laid in late March or early April.

Unfortunately during the breeding season many Canada ganders are spiteful with other geese and ducks and for this reason the paired birds should be kept on their own during the spring and summer.

The Canada Goose is the only goose that really "honks", and to hear two or three pairs calling to each other with their delightful trombone notes back and forth across a lake, is a pleasure not easily forgotten.

Nearly a dozen different races or varieties of the Canada Goose have been described from North America, all differing to a greater or lesser extent in size or colouring. The race known as the "Cackling Goose" from Alaska, alone calls for comment here, as it is so much smaller than most of the others, being about the size of the Barnacle Goose. It is a most attractive bird for a garden or small paddock. *Incubation period 27–30 days.*

THE BARNACLE GOOSE (*Branta leucopsis*) breeds in the Far North, and winters in Britain and northern Europe. This handsome little black, white and grey goose is highly ornamental and should be included in every collection as it does not require too much space. Fortunately there is a good stock of hand-reared birds in this country.

During most of the year the Barnacle Goose will be almost self-supporting if it has plenty of fine short grass for grazing, but during the winter it will require a little help in the way of mash, cooked potatoes, or grain. We have found it quite harmless in the garden, and it does not bully other waterfowl. Both goose and gander have a shrill, yapping note of alarm, pleasure or excitement, while they also have a pleasant conversational mutter.

Hand-reared birds breed freely from their third year, and make excellent parents. They are easily tamed, but are more liable to panic than most geese. *Incubation period 25–28 days.*

THE BRENT GOOSE (*Branta bernicla*). There are two forms of this small dark goose, the light-bellied race breeding in Arctic Canada and in Greenland and Spitzbergen and the dark-bellied race which breeds in Arctic Europe and Asia. Both races winter in the British Isles, where they now enjoy total protection.

There is also an American form known there as the BLACK BRANT, which breeds in Canada and winters on the Pacific shores of America and Asia.

All are attractive birds but are not easy to acquire, although a stock of hand-reared birds is gradually being built up. *Incubation period 21–28 days.*

THE RED-BREASTED GOOSE (*Branta ruficollis*) breeds in Siberia and winters in the neighbourhood of the Caspian Sea.

This exceedingly beautiful little goose is much sought-after for collections, but unfortunately it is both scarce and expensive, and it is by no means easy to obtain birds.

Smaller than the Barnacle Goose, the Red-breasted is coloured black, white and chestnut, in a most curious and distinctive pattern, the bright chestnut-red on face and breast being framed by sharply defined black and white. It has a very small black bill and black legs.

The small stock of Red-breasted Geese in this country before the war, most of which were at Woburn Abbey in Bedfordshire, were shy breeders, and their numbers did not increase to any extent. At the present time there are big flocks at the Wildfowl Trust and Whipsnade, as well as in a number of private collections, but breeding results are still very modest.

Quite harmless with other waterfowl, this goose has the one drawback, that it is extremely noisy during the breeding season. *Incubation period 25–28 days.*

The South American geese or Shelgeese are particularly suitable for keeping on lawns or in paddocks or parks, as they spend much of their time grazing on land, and are quite happy with very little water. Unfortunately the ganders of all species are quarrelsome and vicious with each other, and with other geese and ducks during the breeding season, though they are harmless enough if kept with geese larger than themselves. Ample space is really a necessity for them.

The species most regularly kept in this country are:

THE ANDEAN GOOSE (*Chloëphaga melanoptera*). The sexes of this very striking goose are alike, though the gander is larger. They are white, with black wings and tail and black drop-shaped marks on the mantle. The bill is pink, with a black nail, and the legs are bright red. They are almost entirely terrestrial, being satisfied with only the smallest amount of water for bathing and drinking. They stand very upright and, with their slightly hooked beaks, look more like large birds-of-prey than geese.

Andean Geese are particularly savage with other waterfowl, and must be kept strictly by themselves. They are at present scarce in collections. They are reasonably hardy in this country, but benefit from a warm shed on winter nights. *Incubation period 30 days.*

THE ASHY-HEADED GOOSE (*Chloëphaga poliocephala*). This is a small goose and the sexes differ only in size. They are attractive birds, being a soft grey on head and neck, with a reddish-chestnut breast, white flanks barred with black, black bill and orange and black legs.

In general habits they are typical of all South American geese, being great grazers, quite hardy and very quarrelsome. They breed freely in captivity.

The male has a pleasant trilling note. *Incubation period 30 days.*

THE RUDDY-HEADED GOOSE (*Chloëphaga rubidiceps*). Rather smaller than the previous species, it has a reddish head, brown breast suffused with orange and heavily barred with black, and orange and black legs. In other respects it closely resembles the Ashy-headed Goose. *Incubation period 30 days.*

THE MAGELLAN OR UPLAND GOOSE (*Chloëphaga picta*) is a large and handsome bird, the gander being white and grey, with dark barring on back and flanks and black wings, beak and feet. The female is reddish-buff, heavily barred, with black on the breast and flanks, and with yellow legs. Both sexes have white shoulders and a dark green wing-bar. They are about the size of the Pink-foot, but longer on the leg. There is also a very dark race of this goose in which the male is white, heavily barred with black all over except for the head; the female is also darker.

Magellan Geese become delightfully tame and friendly, and are perfectly hardy in our climate. They breed freely from their third year and the young can safely be left to their parents' care, being reared entirely on grass, though they will eat mash and corn freely. The downy goslings are grey and black and, in first plumage, take after their parents, according to their sex, though the colourings are duller.

Eggs are laid in April and *incubation takes 30 days.*

THE EGYPTIAN GOOSE (*Alopochen aegyptiacus*) is closely related to the Shelducks. A native of Africa, this handsome bird has long been popular with aviculturalists in this country and elsewhere. In some large private parks colonies have been established at complete liberty, and they show little inclination to wander.

They are in every way hardy and easy to maintain, but unfortunately they cannot be kept in a mixed flock with smaller waterfowl, as they are extremely savage and dangerous with smaller ducks and geese. They will fight among themselves during the breeding season, but given sufficient space, a number can be kept together or with the larger geese or swans without danger of serious injury.

A rather pale, greyish-buff with chestnut, black and green wings and pink bill and feet, the Egyptian Goose is a very striking bird under all conditions and particularly against a background of green grass and old park trees. The sexes are practically alike.

Egyptian Geese breed very freely whether at liberty or in confinement, nesting in boxes, drainpipes, hollow trees or ruins, or even under thick bushes. The downy young are dark brown on the back and whitish underneath, very much on the pattern of the young Shelduck. *Incubation period 28–30 days.*

THE ABYSSINIAN BLUE-WINGED GOOSE (*Cyanochen cyanopterus*). Confined in a wild state to the highlands of Abyssinia, this rather sober-plumaged goose is now well represented in waterfowl collections.

Males and females are alike, of medium size, grey-brown in colour except for their striking blue-grey shoulders and green speculum. They are easily tamed and quite hardy but are liable to be quarrelsome and bad tempered with other fowl. *Incubation period about 30 days.*

THE SWAN GOOSE (*Anser cygnoides*). This goose is the ancestor of the domestic Chinese Goose, whereas all other domestic geese spring from the Graylag. It is very similar in appearance to the brown Chinese Goose but has a longer bill and the gander lacks the knob on the bill. Breeds in Siberia and winters in China. In our opinion it is not a very attractive species. *Incubation period 30 days.*

We have not of course tried to describe all the different species of geese from all over the world. There are a number which are still rare in collections, such as the NENE or HAWAIIAN GOOSE, the ORINOCO GOOSE and the KELP GEESE from South America, and others from Africa and Australia.

Most of them are for the specialist only but one which would be worthy of a place in most large collections is the CEREOPSIS or CAPE BARREN GOOSE which comes from Australia.

A handsome and interesting bird of medium size, it is a light grey in colour with black spots on the mantle, a light green bill and pink legs. It hardly ever swims, so requires very little water and is hardy and easy to keep provided it has access to abundant grazing. It becomes extremely tame but unfortunately is rather quarrelsome with other birds. Being a denizen of the Antipodes it usually breeds during our winter months. *Incubation period 35 days.*

CHAPTER 12

THE SWANS

SUITABLE FOR LARGE POND

Swans are probably the most beautiful and decorative of all waterfowl, whatever their surroundings may be, but to be seen at their best they really need complete liberty on a large expanse of water such as a lake or moat or mill-pond, where they can sail in their stately fashion against a background of dark water and tall trees.

Under such conditions, with the addition perhaps of an island or reed-bed for breeding purposes, a pair of swans will be almost self-supporting, except during very severe weather, when they may need extra feeding. During the summer they will prove useful in keeping the pool or lake clear of weeds. They are also fond of grazing.

If there is not sufficient space to allow them full liberty, most swans will do perfectly well if kept on their own in a small enclosure with sufficient swimming water, but it is a mistake to keep them in such a confined area with a mixed flock of waterfowl. To begin with the swans' size makes them appear clumsy alongside ducks and geese, while they are at times, and particularly in the breeding season, liable to be spiteful towards other birds smaller and weaker than themselves.

Wherever they are kept, swans are always interesting and they are hardy, easily tamed and very long-lived—having been recorded as living to be more than a hundred years of age.

Because of their strength and courage, they have few enemies and though an occasional young bird may be slain by a fox or otter, they are on the whole, very capable of looking after themselves under most circumstances, and the majority of human beings have learnt to have a healthy respect for the power of their beak and wings.

When allowed free range on moat or mill-pool, swans will spend a great part of their lives on the water, for their food consists very largely of water-plants and weeds, which they dredge up from below the surface with the aid of their long necks, but where plenty of short grass is available, they will graze almost as freely as do geese.

If confined to a small piece of water in an enclosure where natural food is scarce, swans will take quite readily to a diet of cabbage, lettuce, chopped grass and apples, helped out with a daily ration of corn and household scraps.

Unless an extensive area of water is available, it is unwise to try to keep more than one pair of swans together, or there will be trouble at nesting-time, when territories are being staked out.

Individual birds vary in this respect, but as a rule a pair of swans will stake a claim to an entire lake or mere, and will fight and drive off any other swans that try to share it with them.

On a river or stream, many swans can live together in harmony during the autumn and winter, but when spring comes, each pair generally claims exclusive rights to some quarter of a mile or so of bank, and they will not allow other pairs to trespass.

NESTING

Swans build an elaborate and bulky nest of rushes and water-weed on an island or in a reed-bed, or else on the banks of a stream. The usual number of eggs is from four to seven, but larger clutches are not unusual. The female or "pen", alone incubates, while the male or "cob" mounts guard by the nest, ready to oppose most furiously the approach of an intruder. Communal nesting is not very usual except where the birds have always lived in close proximity to each other, as at the famous Abbotsbury swannery in Dorset, which is almost unique in that respect.

Those who wish to introduce swans to a piece of water for the first time would be well advised to start with a pair of adults or well-grown cygnets, rather than try to obtain a sitting of eggs, for young cygnets are not easy to rear, particularly under hens, as they like to feed on the water. A domestic goose makes a better foster-mother but generally speaking, all swans should be left to rear their own young.

Cygnets, aided by their parents, will generally find most of their own food but they will also enjoy chopped lettuce if scattered on the water near them and they and the old birds will also take biscuit-meal, bread and household scraps.

Swans are powerful and ready flyers and newly-acquired birds should always be wing-clipped until they have settled down and become attached to their new home, after which they will generally stay in the vicinity for the rest of their days. They are supposed to mate for life.

THE MUTE SWAN (*Cygnus olor*) is the common semi-domesticated bird of our public parks, rivers and lakes, where it fends for for itself almost entirely except in very severe weather when it is always quite ready to accept human bounty. A "feral" strain has become established on many rivers and broads and on some of our salt-water estuaries. These birds have become completely independent of man though they are still reasonably tame and confiding.

The Mute Swan is found as a completely wild bird in parts of central and northern Europe, where it is as shy and wary as any truly wild swan. Wild Mute Swans probably inhabited Britain in ancient times.

The Mute Swan can be told from other swans by its large size and orange and black bill, with a conspicuous black knob at the base. The fact that they carry their necks in a graceful S curve is characteristic, as all other swans hold their necks much more erect and straight.

Though their name suggests that they are silent birds Mute Swans actually have a number of calls, from a pleasant bugling note sometimes heard when a number are assembled together, to the husky grunt of the "cob" swan as he swims towards an intruder.

These swans are fearless birds and on their own element, the adults have few enemies except man, though the young are sometimes taken by otters.

Mute Swans cannot rise easily from land or water, but have to beat along the surface, using their large paddles to gain momentum, but once they become air-borne their flight is immensely powerful, while the sound of their wings, which can be heard from afar, has been likened to the galloping of a horse on a hard road.

The nest, which is often used year after year, is a huge struc- ture of dead rushes and water-weeds, turf and twigs, and takes a considerable time to build. The eggs usually number between four and seven, but as many as twelve have been recorded. When first hatched, the cygnets are clad in dirty-grey down, and have greyish feet and bills. Their first plumage too, is grey-brown, and they do not assume their completely white plumage and the knob on their bill until their third year.

The incubation period is about five weeks.

THE WHOOPER SWAN (*Cygnus cygnus*) and BEWICK'S SWAN (*Cygnus bewickii*) are the only wild species which occur in this country. Both are winter visitors, though the Whooper also breeds in small numbers in northern Scotland. Both species are white when adult and have lemon-yellow and black bills, without any trace of a knob, and both carry their long, thin necks very erect when swimming.

The Whooper is a large bird, nearly as large as a Mute, and gets its name from the very beautiful whooping notes which it utters both when swimming and in flight. The sound of a flock of Whoopers in flight or circling down to join others on the water, is quite delightful, particularly when heard against the background of some dark, Highland loch.

Bewick's is considerably smaller than the Whooper, with a shorter and thicker neck, and the yellow colour on the bill is very much less extensive. When wintering in Britain, Bewick's Swans seem to prefer our sea coasts and river estuaries, while the Whooper is to be found chiefly on lochs and meres inland.

Both these swans do well in confinement, even in a restricted space and the Whooper has bred quite frequently under such conditions. They are less quarrelsome than the Mute, but breeding pairs should be kept by themselves. Single birds alone are usually quite harmless with other fowl.

Bewick's Swan is probably the more interesting and desirable of the two species, but neither are common in captivity at the present time, and although a hand-reared strain has been established, such birds are still scarce.

The incubation period of both species varies to a certain extent, but can be *taken to be between five and six weeks.*

THE BLACK SWAN (*Cygnus atratus*) is a native of Australia, where it is still quite plentiful in a wild state. Introduced into Europe some 150 years ago, it is now a familiar bird in Zoos and some private collections.

It is one of the most attractive and desirable of all the swans, but is unfortunately savage with other waterfowl and needs to be kept separate from other birds. Nor should black swans be left full-winged as they are given to wandering. On the other hand they are quite content with a much smaller area of water than are most of the other swans and they have, in fact been recorded as breeding successfully in a pen that contained no swimming water at all.

This swan is completely hardy in our climate and requires much the same food and treatment as the commoner species. They breed very freely in captivity and not infrequently lay two clutches of eggs in a year. They are excellent parents, both sexes taking part in the incubation of the eggs and care of the young cygnets.

The Black Swan is smaller than the Mute Swan. It has dark sooty-brown plumage with pale edges to most of the feathers. It has white flight feathers, while most of the wing-coverts have curiously curved edges to the feathers. The bill is bright red, with a white band across it and the iris is also bright red. The legs are black.

When hatched the cygnets are clad in greyish-white down and their first plumage is grey-brown, spotted with white. They do not assume complete adult dress until after their second moult.

Incubation period about five weeks.

The only other swans with which we need concern ourselves here, both come from South America. They are both interesting and ornamental birds but at present are rare in collections and therefore expensive to buy.

THE COSCOROBA (*Coscoroba coscoroba*) is quite small, little larger than some geese and is also most goose-like in its habits since it likes to graze on short grass rather than dredge up water-weeds as the other swans do. It is pure white with some black on the primary feathers and has a pink bill and pink feet. It is reasonably hardy and far less of a bully than other swans, so can safely be kept in a mixed collection of wildfowl.

THE BLACK-NECKED SWAN (*C. melanocoryphus*) is also highly ornamental but the species is still scarce in collections and rather expensive to buy. It is a less spiteful bird than the Mute or the Black Swan and seldom attacks ducks or geese apart from the Common Shelduck which somewhat resembles it in colour.

When two or three years old, this swan will frequently lay two clutches of eggs each season. The old birds make excellent parents, looking after their young with the greatest care. The latter take to the water almost as soon as they are hatched, and when tired they will climb up on to their parents' backs while on the water, tucking themselves away for warmth amid their back feathers. Both cob and pen will thus carry their young.

The adult Black-necked Swan has white body plumage with a velvety black head and neck and flesh-coloured legs and feet. Perhaps its most noticeable and attractive feature, however, is the blue bill with a large bright red knob at the base. The young in down are yellow, and in first plumage are greyish with light brown necks.

The incubation period for both the above species is about five weeks.

CHAPTER 13

ORNAMENTAL DOMESTIC DUCKS

UTILITY PROPERTIES

Is is probably not generally known that in addition to the large variety of ornamental wildfowl that are now kept in confinement, there are several breeds of domestic ducks which are also distinctly ornamental.

Three of these domestic breeds are officially classified as "ornamental" by the Poultry Club of Great Britain and the British Waterfowl Association, i.e. the Black East Indian Duck, the Decoy or Call Duck and the Silver Appleyard Bantam Duck.

This does not mean, of course, that no other breeds of domestic ducks are ornamental but that they are not so termed for exhibition purposes and do not have a "Standard of Perfection" laid down for their class at poultry shows. These others would, therefore, have to be entered in the "Other Variety of Duck" Class, instead of in the "Ornamental" Class.

Although perhaps not quite so interesting to keep as wild birds, these domestic breeds have definite advantages over the former in that they are very tame and easy to rear, lay considarably more eggs and are cheaper to buy in the first place. They are all extremely hardy and are unsurpassed as cleaners of waterweed from moats and ponds. In addition they make very good table birds.

A small flock of any of the three breeds of domestic ornamental ducks would be particularly suitable for a farm pond or mill pond or a pair or two would do well on a small artificial pool. On the other hand they can also be kept in an ordinary wired-in pen, as they do not need much water for swimming.

All three breeds are free-flyers unless pinioned or wing-clipped. The eggs, which have a high fertility rate, can be hatched by the ducks themselves, under hens or bantams or in incubators, and the ducklings are as easy to rear as other domestic breeds. They can also be used as foster-mothers for the rarer waterfowl ducklings, as they make good sitters and gentle competent mothers and being very confiding with human beings, do not drag their young all over the place in the way wild ducks so often do.

The most interesting of the three recognized ornamental breeds is THE DECOY or CALL DUCK. This breed originated in Holland where they are used extensively in the commercial duck decoys for enticing wild duck into the decoys by their loud and continuous quacking. In France they are called "Mignon" Ducks and are kept largely for decorative purposes.

Standards are laid down for the two colour varieties, White and Brown, whilst Pied, Silver and Blue varieties are now obtainable also. The White Call Duck should be small and compact, pure white in colour with orange bill, legs and feet. The head should be well rounded and the beak short and broad. The Brown Call Duck should be similar in size and shape but coloured like the Mallard. *Incubation period 28 days.*

THE BLACK EAST INDIAN DUCK is rather larger than the Call Duck and if of a good strain is very striking in appearance. Both sexes are black with a vivid beetle-green gloss to the feathers, the drake being brighter than the duck. As there is considerable Mallard blood in their make-up, the drakes have the characteristic up-curled tail feathers of the former.

The Black East Indian lays well, the first eggs laid being almost black, later ones grey and finally all eggs are normal duck-egg colour. One drake should be kept with three or four ducks. This breed is possibly the best of all for clearing ponds and streams of unsightly weeds and its flesh makes excellent eating. *Incubation period 28 days.*

THE SILVER APPLEYARD BANTAM DUCK is a delightful little bird, only slightly larger than a Call Duck, trim and neat in appearance and of a friendly disposition. They are attractively mottled and striped with fawn, brown and grey on a white background, while the drake has a greenish head colouring when in full dress. S.A.B.'s as they are often termed, are excellent layers and good table birds. *Incubation period 28 days.*

PLATE 18

Photo : Richard Burn

A MIXED COLLECTION. SHINGLE WHICH CAN BE RAKED REGULARLY PREVENTS THE VERGE
FROM BECOMING MUDDY

PLATE 19

Photo : Rigden & Hodge Ltd.

A PAIR OF BLACK SWANS WITH CYGNETS

PLATE 20

Photo : Christina Sanday

BLACK-NECKED SWANS

PLATE 21

Photo : Richard Burn

SOME ORNAMENTAL DOMESTIC DUCKS. BLACK EAST INDIAN (on flanks), WHITE CALL DUCKS (left centre), SILVER APPLEYARD BANTAM (right centre)

A number of other domestic ducks are ornamental in appearance though they do not qualify as such for exhibition purposes. They are:

THE SILVER APPLEYARD DUCK. This is a much enlarged version of the S.A.B. already mentioned and deserves to be more widely known, being nice to look at, a very good layer of large eggs and a really first-class table bird.

THE CAYUGA is, in the same way, a large edition of the Black East Indian Duck but is even more brightly coloured. This makes them one of the favourite exhibits at poultry shows. In some people's opinion they are the best eating of all domestic ducks, not excluding the famous Aylesburys.

THE BUFF ORPINGTON DUCK has been in existence for some sixty years. It was originally bred by a Mr. Cook of Orpington, Kent, who also produced the chicken of the same name. It is decorative in a modest way, being a rich reddish-buff. The drake has a glossy seal-brown head. They are good layers and good table birds. All these domestic ducks have an *incubation period of about 28 days.*

THE MUSCOVY DUCK, a large and rather ungainly bird, is the common domestic duck of South America, Australia and tropical Africa. It only occurs as a wild species in parts of central America where it nests in the tops of high trees in the old nests of birds of prey. The domestic breed has to a certain extent inherited the habit for it likes to nest on tops of stacks or thatched buildings. It also perches freely on roofs and trees.
Some people consider Muscovies ornamental, others do not. The wild bird is almost entirely black, with some white on the wings, but domestic birds can be of many colours, pure white, black or a mixture of both and there is a very attractive lavender and white variety.
Both sexes have a patch of bare red skin round the eyes and the drake has a slight crest and a fleshy knob at the base of the bill. The latter is a large bird often weighing as much as twelve pounds, but the duck is only about half this size. They have no quack, the drake expressing its feelings with a curious puffing noise and a see-saw motion of the head.
Muscovy Ducks are definitely birds of character and make charming pets. They are strong if rather ponderous flyers and have a pronounced homing instinct. The duck lays a good number of eggs in spring and summer and she also makes an excellent foster-mother for the larger kinds of waterfowl. The young make excellent table birds, particularly if crossed with other domestic ducks. *Incubation period 35 days.*

INCUBATION PERIOD (IN DAYS)
OF SOME WATERFOWL
(All are subject to slight variation)

SWANS

Bewick's, 34–38
Black, 34–37
Black-necked, 34–36
Coscoroba, 35
Mute, 35–38
Whooper, 35–42

GEESE

Abyssinian Blue-winged, 30
Andean, 30
Ashy-headed, 30
Bar-headed, 28–30
Barnacle, 25–28
Bean, 27–30
Brent, 25–28
Canada, 27–30
Cereopsis, 35
Egyptian, 28–30
Emperor, 26–28 (usually 27)
Greylag, 27–30
Lesser White-fronted, 25–28
Magellan, 30
Maned, 28
Pink-footed, 25–28
Red-breasted, 25–28
Ruddy-headed, 30
Snow, 24–28
Swan Goose, 30
White-fronted, 28–30

ORNAMENTAL DOMESTIC DUCKS

Black East Indian, 28
Buff Orpington, 28
Decoy Duck, 28
Muscovy, 35
Silver Appleyard Bantam Duck, 28

DUCKS

Argentine Red Shoveler, 23
Australian Wood, 28
Bahama Pintail, 25
Baikal Teal, 23–25
Blue-winged Teal, 23
Brazilian Teal, 25
Cape Teal, 25–26
Carolina, 28–30
Chestnut-breasted Teal, 27
Chilean Teal, 25–26
Chiloe Wigeon, 25
Cinnamon Teal, 23
Common Pintail, 23
Common Pochard, 25
Common Shelduck, 28
Common Teal, 23
Falcated Teal, 26
Gadwall, 23–24
Garganey, 23
Laysan Teal, 25
Mallard, 28
Mandarin, 28–30
Red-crested Pochard, 25–26
Rosybill, 25–26
Ruddy Shelduck, 28–29
Scaup, 28
Shoveler, 23
South African Shelduck, 29–30
Spotbill, 26
Tufted, 25–26
Wigeon, 25

INDEX

INDEX